# GRAVEN IMAGES:

*Substitutes for True Morality*

Also by Dietrich von Hildebrand

# GRAVEN IMAGES:

*Substitutes for True Morality*

By DIETRICH VON HILDEBRAND
with ALICE JOURDAIN

FRANCISCAN HERALD PRESS
1434 WEST 51st STREET ● CHICAGO, 60609

*Nihil Obstat:*
JOHN A. GOODWINE, J.C.D.
*Censor Librorum*

*Imprimatur:*
✠ FRANCIS CARDINAL SPELLMAN
ARCHBISHOP OF NEW YORK

*January 4, 1957*

The nihil obstat and imprimatur are official declarations that a book or pamphlet is free of doctrinal or moral error. No implication is contained therein that those who have granted the nihil obstat and imprimatur agree with the contents, opinions or statements expressed.

**Library of Congress Cataloging in Publication Data**

Von Hildebrand, Dietrich, 1880-
    Graven images.

    Reprint of the 1957 ed. published by McKay, New York.
    1. Ethics. I. Von Hildebrand, Alice M. Jourdain, joint author. II. Title.
BJ37.V6  1976      170      76-965
ISBN 0-8199-0597-6

# Contents

# GRAVEN IMAGES:

## *Substitutes for True Morality*

## CHAPTER I

# THE NATURE OF SUBSTITUTES

THERE ARE VARIOUS notions which function as the decisive
moral standards and norms in the life of both individuals
and communities, such as honor, the notion of "the gentleman," the *bien pensant,* etc. One opposes the decent man to
the "good for nothing," the efficient man to the stumblebum,
the loyal to the disloyal.

The striking point is that for many people those different
norms function as substitutes for the categories of the morally
good and evil. In all those norms, there is a moral connotation, and yet they all contain also an extra-moral element.
The man who is ready to endure anything rather than stain
his honor will not shrink from certain immoral attitudes and
actions, provided they are not incompatible with his honor.[1]
Another who will abstain from any act of disloyalty against
the law of the land, even to the point of sacrifice, will not
draw back from impurity.

All these people admit a norm above them to which they

[1] Cf. Tolstoi: "Vronsky's life had been especially happy, because he had
a special code of rules, which infallibly determined all he ought to do and
ought not to do.

"This code embraced a very small circle of duties, but the rules allowed
no manner of question and as Vronsky never had occasion to go outside
of this circle, he had never been obliged to hesitate about what he had to
do. These rules prescribed unfailingly that it was necessary to pay gambling
debts, but not his tailor's bills; that it was not permissible to tell lies, except
to women; that it was not right to deceive anyone except a husband; that
insults could be committed, but never pardoned.

"All these precepts might be wrong and illogical, but they were indubitable;
and in fulfilling them Vronsky felt that he was calm, and had the right
to hold his head high." *Anna Karenina,* translated by N. H. Dole, Vol.
II, p. 91.

want to conform, which in one way or another challenges their conscience; they clearly differ from a man who is completely dominated either by concupiscence or by pride, or by both, and who consequently balks at admitting any norm above himself which imposes on him an obligation to do certain things, and to abstain from others.[2]

Thus all these substitutes, in a largely differentiated scale, include still some faint reflection of the natural moral law. On the other hand, they all include some perversion of the moral law. If we are to understand the nature of these substitutes for morality, we must realize that they all preserve the most formal *eidos* of the moral sphere, and therefore differ thoroughly from all ideals and idols which are antithetical to morality.

Consequently, our first task will be to distinguish between substitutes for morality and anti- or a-moral ideals.

## A. Substitutes and Anti-moral Ideals

When we think of Nietzsche's *Umwertung der Werte*, we see that his ideal of the "superman" is a clear-cut declaration of war on morality in its most formal *eidos*. He wants to do away with the most formal character of the morally good and evil; he rejects a norm above ourselves which would oblige us to obey and which would appeal to our conscience; he wants to "liberate" man, by ousting the notion of guilt. He wants to replace morality, as such, by something radically amoral, which even in its most formal character has nothing in common with morality.

Yet the formal notion of value is maintained,[3] for Nietzsche claims his "superman" to be endowed with values. He does not praise his "superman" merely from the point of view of

---

[2] These people thus clearly differ from the radically amoral and immoral man who rejects any norm whatever.

[3] Nietzsche even introduces the term "value" and it cannot be denied that in this term a certain philosophical *prise de conscience* of the important-in-itself is embodied.

the objective good for the person, nor from that of the merely subjectively satisfying. Though he does not make these distinctions and ignores them *de facto,* he tacitly claims his "superman" to be endowed with values, i.e., with importance-in-itself. Prescinding from the question whether or not the "blond beast" really embodies authentic extra-moral values, it is indubitable that Nietzsche claims the "superman" to be endowed with high values. The formal category of importance-in-itself is in question. Yet this does in no way make it a substitute for morality. The moral values form a domain of their own in the realm of values, as we have pointed out in *Christian Ethics.*[4] And the difference between moral values and all other qualitative and ontological values is an extremely deep and important one. We have stated before [5] that it is not only a qualitative difference, but a difference of theme. The different families or domains of qualitative values —such as the intellectual, the aesthetic, and the moral—are distinguished by their basic theme. It is of the utmost importance in our context to elaborate the formal *eidos* of the theme proper to moral values, and its unique character and role with respect to all other themes of values. This theme obviously also extends to all morally relevant values which do not coincide with the moral values themselves, as we saw. But their moral relevance implies a deep intrinsic connection with the moral theme, their call addressed to us is pervaded by that theme; it is only among them that we find the unique type of obligation which is the moral obligation.

Nietzsche in presenting his "superman" as an embodiment of certain values in no way claims the "superman" to be endowed with moral values. His thesis is precisely to deny the very existence of moral values, and of the moral theme, and to interpret it as an idol of *ressentiment.* He declares war on the moral sphere and theme as such, and *replaces* it

4 Dietrich von Hildebrand, *Christian Ethics* (New York: David McKay Company, Inc., 1953) , Chapter 15.
5 *Ibid.,* Chapter 10.

consciously by extra-moral values, by an extra-moral theme.[6] And this precisely reveals that his "superman" is not a substitute for morality; for we saw above that every substitute for morality—though a distortion and perversion of the moral theme—still retains some features of the most general *eidos* of the moral theme. Apart from this fundamental difference, we may still add that in Nietzsche's case we are confronted with a philosophical theory, whereas the substitutes, as we saw, are more or less the lived norms and standards of communities and individuals.

Another example of an anti-moral theory which would oust morality, instead of substituting for it, is the hedonism of Aristippus of Cyrene. In claiming that the subjectively satisfying, as the only real category of importance, should be the only norm for our actions, the most formal moral theme is expressly rejected and declared to be an illusion. Though this theory arrogates to itself the title of "ethics," it is even more remote from the moral theme than Nietzsche's ideal, because it denies not only the moral values but any value. According to Aristippus, there exists no importance-in-itself. He replaces morality, not with an extra-moral value, but with the merely subjectively satisfying. Nietzsche's "superman," though antithetical to morality and intended to be such, can still be called a false ideal or idol; hedonism is no ideal at all, and does not even claim to be one. Aristippus, it is true, inevitably introduces the notion of value or the important-in-itself in the idea of the "wise man," who is precisely the one who accepts no norm, except the subjectively satisfying, and who applies this norm consistently and according to its immanent logic. But the notion of the "wise man" has nothing of the substitute character for morality which it has in the Cynic or the Stoic philosophy. To seek pleasure in a reasonable manner is definitely not a norm which addresses itself to our conscience, which obliges us, and makes us feel

---

[6] We are concerned here only with Nietzsche's intention. In fact, he is bound to reintroduce moral values tacitly, as does everyone who denies them.

guilty if we do not conform to it. Failure to conform is here not a matter of wickedness, but of foolishness.

The same applies to a strict and consistent Machiavellism. He who says that we should not care whether something is morally good or evil, but only whether it is expedient or not, deprives the "should" of any moral connotation; and his theory openly and *expressis verbis* ousts morality. It is not the declaration of war on morality as in Nietzsche's ideal, but a more or less cynical ignoring of the moral sphere, looking at the moral sphere and moral theme as something belonging rather in the realm of superstition and deprived of any validity. In this case, we can no longer speak of an ideal at all.

The specific nature of the substitutes for morality comes still more clearly to the fore when we compare the substitutes with amoral ideals which nevertheless imply the datum of values, such as Nietzsche's "superman" or aestheticism.

The aesthete, for whom the only real value is beauty in nature and art, and who considers the moral sphere as something indifferent, clearly differs from one who adheres to a moral substitute, the man of honor, for example, or the "gentleman."

Form beauty [7] alone plays a decisive role in his life. It is the one measure which he applies in judging all matters and for which he will make sacrifices. Indeed it is the only thing which he considers to be serious. But this ideal has none of the features of the most general *eidos* of morality. It does not challenge the conscience of the aesthete; it does not impose obligations on him which could be compared with the moral obligation. He feels no guilt when he fails to conform to this ideal. Far from it, for has he not done away with the moral sphere as something obsolete? Indeed, he feels superior to morality which may bind the average man, the uncultivated herd, but not the refined, cultured man that he feels himself to be. Beauty in art and nature and

[7] Dietrich von Hildebrand, *The New Tower of Babel* (New York: P. J. Kenedy, 1953), pp. 183-202.

aesthetic values of all kinds are for him not substitutes for morality; their role in his life, great as it may be, differs completely, even in its most formal aspect, from the one which the moral sphere by its very nature plays.

## B. SUBSTITUTES AND PATHOLOGICAL DEFORMATIONS

We must further distinguish the substitutes from different pathological deformations of the moral sphere.

Inhibitions of all kinds are well-known phenomena. The experience of an irrational obstacle, hindering us from doing something which as such we would like to do, differs to such an extent from the experience of a moral prohibition that only someone who is blind to the nature and essence of the given can confuse the two.

When our conscience warns us against doing something (warning which is based on a clear, rational understanding of the moral disvalue of an attitude), this experience differs from the irrational, purely psychological inhibition, as the intrinsic necessity of a *veritas aeterna* differs from the psychological "must" of an *idée fixe*.

An abyss yawns between the irrationally blunt, merely factual character of the inhibition and the axiological character of the moral prohibition which is given in its objective validity. The former is moreover a purely psychological hindrance; the latter, on the contrary, is an objective commandment rooted in a moral or morally relevant disvalue. The former is a handicap to our freedom; the latter, on the contrary, appeals to our free response and calls for a free refusal of the morally evil action.

In every formal or material respect, the inhibition obviously differs from any moral prohibition. It is thus clear that inhibitions also completely differ from any substitute. The substitute presents itself also as endowed with an objective "oughtness." It represents the moral sphere, though inadequately; it has an axiological and rational character and appeals to the conscience and free will of the person.

Like the inhibition, "pathological bondage" in relation to someone else has no moral character, and therefore cannot be interpreted as a substitute in our sense. Some persons are submitted to others by an irrational dependence; they are in the power of others, as though hypnotized by them. This dependence, which manifests itself in a sham obedience toward the commands of another, clearly differs from submission to a true authority—a submission which we recognize as due to authority. In one case we have an irrational dependence which curtails our freedom, paralyzes our free decision, and has the character of a mere factual power; in the other case we have a free, luminous response, based on clear insight into the true character of authority and the moral duty to obey.

Yet, radically different as any pathological restraint or compulsion is from moral obligation, there are cases in which the two are interwoven. In certain persons, the awareness of a moral obligation assumes the pathological character of a psychological coercion. Their neurosis is such that even a moral obligation, though so thoroughly different from any pathological compulsion, generates an irrational pressure, and acts on them in a way which contradicts its very nature.

Yet this perversion is also patently completely different from the substitute. In the neurotic man, moral obligations create inhibitions in a psychological manner; but the coercion or inhibition does not represent the moral sphere in a conscious, rational manner. The moral obligation creates here something amoral, something psychological which is mixed with moral elements; but this mixture is not an extra-moral value which illegitimately assumes the place of the morally good. It is not, as in the case of substitutes, another qualitative or formal notion which represents the moral sphere; but is, rather, a perversion of the experience of moral obligation which assumes the character of a psychological coercion.

The difference between these kinds of pathological perversion and the substitutes for morality is manifested in the case of the scrupulous man who feels himself guilty even when there is no question of guilt; who sees moral obligations where there are none and always fears that he has overlooked some; and who, when shown that he has not sinned, doubts that others have really grasped the case. The perversion here in question is clearly no substitute. It is, on the one hand, an egocentrism, an introversion, and on the other, a pathological mistrust and anxiety. But it clearly differs from any substitute and can be found both in persons who set up a substitute as moral norm, and in persons who adhere to the true moral norm. The perversion does not refer to another notion replacing the true moral norm, but to the state of mind in which one approaches the moral sphere.

The specific characteristic of this type of perversion is that the pathological aberration is restricted to the moral sphere. It is not a general inhibition extended to the moral sphere, but a kind of allergy to the moral sphere, a state of mind which reacts pathologically to anything moral or religious.

This may suffice to show that the entire sphere of pathological deformations of morality clearly differs from the substitutes and is thus excluded from our topic.

CHAPTER II

# SUBSTITUTES AND OTHER MORAL
# DEFORMATIONS

Now THAT WE HAVE distinguished the substitutes for morality
from amoral or anti-moral idols, as well as from pathological
deformations of the moral sphere, we must elaborate further
the nature of the substitutes for morality. We begin with the
distinction between the substitutes and other types of deformations within the moral sphere.

## A. GENERAL VALUE BLINDNESS AND MORAL VALUE BLINDNESS

We discussed in *Christian Ethics* [1] and in a former work [2]
the relation between pride and concupiscence on the one
hand, and value blindness on the other, i.e., especially the
blindness to moral values.

The man dominated by satanic pride is totally value-blind,
i.e., pride bars from his sight the very nature of the important-
in-itself. Yet, in contradistinction to the brutelike concupiscent man who is also completely value-blind, he is aware
of the metaphysical "throne" [3] of all values. Because of this
"throne," he sees in all values a rival to his own superiority;

---

[1] Cf. Chapters 34 and 35.

[2] Dietrich von Hildebrand, *Sittlichkeit und ethische Werterkenntniss*
(Halle: M. Niemeyer, 1921).

[3] Cf. *Christian Ethics:* "The man who has fallen prey to this satanic pride
is blind to the real nature of values, to their intrinsic beauty and dignity,
but, unlike the concupiscent man, who in his complete bluntness ignores
values, he grasps their metaphysical power. Certainly he misunderstands
the nature of this metaphysical power, otherwise he could not attempt to
dissociate it from values. He sees the metaphysical "throne" of values and
simultaneously he misses the very nature of this "throne." P. 443.

and, as a result, he wages war against them, and ultimately against God, their Source.

But it must be emphasized that, although the satanically proud man is blind to all values and grasps only their metaphysical "throne," what he really hates are the *moral* values, reflecting God in a unique manner. The real antithesis is between moral values and pride,[4] precisely because pride is ultimately directed against God.

This fact becomes even clearer when we turn to the non-metaphysical type of pride,[5] which we find embodied in a Don Juan [6] and in Don Rodrigo.[7] Here we find a downright, hostile attitude to the moral sphere and a blindness to moral values, but neither a blindness to extra-moral values nor a hostile attitude toward them.

Don Juan understands that intellectual brilliance is a value and that courage and self-domination are values; he is aware of the "throne" of these values, and consequently wishes to possess them. Although his understanding of the value character of these qualities is limited and distorted, although his response to them in other persons differs thoroughly from the authentic value response, he nevertheless grasps not only the "throne" proper to these values, he even has some awareness of their preciousness. Thus the fundamental difference between moral values and extra-moral values, in their relation to pride, comes clearly to the fore. Don Juan is radically blind to moral values and the moral significance of all morally relevant values; he has a hostile attitude toward the moral sphere, and does not even perceive the metaphysical "throne" of the moral values (as does the satanically proud). Consequently, he does not aspire to their possession as a source of superiority. But, as we have seen,

---

[4] The same applies analogously to concupiscence. The real antithesis is between moral values and concupiscence.

[5] Cf. *Christian Ethics*, p. 434 ff.

[6] The main personage in Mozart's opera of the same name.

[7] A personage in Manzoni's novel, *The Betrothed*.

he is not necessarily blind to extra-moral values, and many of them he even aspires to possess. Thus we see that a man in whom the loving, humble, reverent center is completely overshadowed by pride and concupiscence, who can in no way be considered as a man in whom the humble, loving, value-responding center on the one hand, and pride and concupiscence on the other, coexist, is not necessarily blind to extra-moral values.[8]

The fact that the real antithesis is to be found between moral values on the one hand, and pride and concupiscence on the other, manifests itself also in another direction.

In *Christian Ethics,* we mentioned three different types of men. First, the type in whom the value-responding, loving center has victoriously silenced pride and concupiscence, and reduced their role to a mere potential one. Such is the case in the saint.

Secondly, the type in whom pride and concupiscence on the one hand, and the value-responding, loving center on the other, coexist. This coexistence can have many different forms, as we also discussed in *Christian Ethics.*[9]

Thirdly, the type in whom pride or concupiscence or both together have silenced the reverent, loving, value-responding center. There certainly always remains the possibility of a conversion. The loving, reverent, value-responding center

8 An especially surprising case of pride is the pharisee. Unlike the satanically proud man who wages war on all values, who never seeks to satisfy his pride by possessing them, and unlike a Don Juan dominated by pride and concupiscence, who in his blindness to moral values does not seek their possession as a source of superiority, the pharisee grasps moral values as a source of a higher superiority and wishes to be endowed by them. He not only comprehends their "throne" and the superiority of their "throne" with respect to extra-moral values, he also sees that their "throne" is incomparably superior to the "throne" of extra-moral values—he understands something of the quality of moral values. What we have here is a radically different way of being poisoned by pride. Cf. Dietrich von Hildebrand with Alice Jourdain, *True Morality and Its Counterfeits* (New York: David McKay Company, Inc., 1955).

9 Cf. Chapter 32.

is still potentially present. In the frame of this third type (i.e., of the definitely amoral and anti-moral man), the fact again comes to the fore that the acme of antitheses to pride and concupiscence is to be found in moral values.

The characteristic mark of this third type in whom pride and concupiscence have silenced the moral value-responding center is in one's position toward moral values and the moral sphere, not one's position toward extra-moral values. The person of this type is not necessarily blind to all values, but always to moral values. He does not necessarily have either a completely indifferent attitude or a hostile attitude toward *all* values, but he is *always* either indifferent or hostile to moral values.

Thus we have to oppose to all forms of coexistence not only the extreme cases of satanical pride and brutelike concupiscence, but also the cases of all those who have a definitely amoral or anti-moral attitude.[10]

Though the main interest in our context is focused on the cases of coexistence, in the frame of which we find the various substitutes for morality, this clarification concerning the definitely amoral man is important for us. It illustrates the fact that the very core of the challenge to pride and concupiscence is not values as such but *moral* values and thus throws into relief one of our main topics, namely, the matchless position of the moral sphere and the unique challenge of moral values—so essentially different from the call of all extra-moral values. Later on we shall come back to this problem, when the role of extra-moral values in the process of building up substitutes for morality is analyzed.

---

10 We cannot, however, assume that this is everywhere the case where a theoretical anti-moral attitude is to be found. In Nietzsche, for instance, we find a theoretical anti-moral idol, which certainly has its roots in his personality, but *de facto* he was neither a Don Rodrigo nor a Richard III, as conceived by Shakespeare.

## B. Traditional Moral Value Blindness and Moral Blindness Due to Pride and Concupiscence

After stating the fundamental difference between value blindness in general and moral value blindness, we must now concentrate on different forms of moral value blindness.

First, we want to make a basic distinction between partial moral value blindness which is due to the influence of pride and concupiscence and partial moral blindness which is due to tradition and education. If we encounter a man who is blind to the moral disvalue of impurity, though he clearly sees the moral disvalue of murder or dishonesty, the role of concupiscence is easily detected—the unconscious barrier created by concupiscence, the unreadiness of the will to overcome concupiscence. Tom Jones [11] does not grasp the horror of impurity, though he certainly is aware of the immorality of murder or of betraying a friend; and we must attribute his blindness not to education but to an unreadiness to fight against his concupiscence.

If we think, on the contrary, of a Mohammedan woman's blindness to the moral disvalue of polygamy, it is easy to see that this blindness is due to the influence of education and tradition. By education and tradition, she has been taught that polygamy is morally unobjectionable. She does not gain any advantage from polygamy; on the contrary, this institution is disadvantageous to her in every respect; it is not concupiscence which blinds her to the moral disvalue of polygamy. Her blindness is due to tradition and education. Polygamy is so much a part of her environment that it is taken for granted. Its moral legitimacy is questioned as little as that of sleeping.

In the frame of the first type of partial moral value blindness, i.e., the moral value blindness due to partial imprisonment in pride and concupiscence, we have further to distinguish the following cases:

[11] Hero in Fielding's novel of the same name.

For the most part, partial moral value blindness refers to such moral values which are more difficult to grasp. The sublimer the moral value, the higher the moral standard which is required in order to grasp the value. It is easier to comprehend the immorality of homicide than the immorality of impurity; it is easier to grasp the immorality of theft than the immorality of pretentious ambition or of pride. One is not surprised to find that in certain peoples murder and theft are considered to be evil, whereas polygamy is viewed as morally unobjectionable. We are not surprised when Aristotle praises the proud man, though he clearly sees so many other moral values and disvalues.[12]

Thus we may say that in most cases, partial moral value blindness refers to those moral values which are objectively more difficult to grasp. The limitation in the grasping and understanding of moral values runs parallel to the hierarchy of values: *the higher the value ranks, the more must the person free himself from the fetters of pride and concupiscence in order to understand it.*[13]

But there exist also other types of partial moral value blindness in which this parallelism is not to be found. Raskolnikov in Dostoevski's novel, *Crime and Punishment,* has a deep understanding of the immorality of impurity; he abhors the pharisaism of Lushin; he has a deep charity for Marmeladoff; but he does not understand the sacredness of every human life. He believes that killing an evil, mean creature, such as his victim was, is no worse than killing lice. There is no doubt that before the murder he really

[12] Nor is it surprising to us that the most sublime virtues are only grasped as a result of the Christian Revelation, because certain virtues are only possible as responses to the God of Christian Revelation, to Christ, and to the world in the light of Christ.

[13] This applies only to the hierarchy of qualitative values. There exists also a hierarchical order of goods referring to the question of the extent to which a value is embodied in a good. With respect to this hierarchical order, the above-mentioned principle does not apply.

The entire problem of the hierarchy of goods, and the difference between these two hierarchical orders, will be analyzed in a later publication.

succeeds in convincing himself of the moral legitimacy of murdering this old woman. This value blindness clearly differs from the above-mentioned type. It does not correspond to the objective order of difficulty in grasping moral values. Whereas Raskolnikov is able to understand the more sublime moral values, requiring a higher moral standard and moral differentiation, he is blind to the more obvious morally relevant value of the sacredness of the life of man.

But this value blindness also differs from the value blindness of a Tom Jones: it is determined by a theory; it has an intellectual character rather than the character of a blindness in the realm of immediate experience. Raskolnikov, having undergone the influence of certain theories in a purely intellectual process, has come to the conclusion that it is cowardice alone that keeps him from killing this obnoxious insect, whose money he could use for great and useful purposes. This theoretical moral value blindness must be clearly distinguished from the real, immediate moral value blindness. The screen hiding the moral or morally relevant value or disvalue is here erected by an erroneous theory, which contradicts the result of immediate value-grasping and which has the effect of leading the victim or creator of this theory to disbelieve what his immediate value-grasping tells him. It is a perversion in the realm of conviction, not of the capacity for perceiving moral values. This becomes obvious when we realize that Raskolnikov, after committing the crime, experiences the horror of his deed, the terrible weight on his conscience, and tries desperately to relieve himself of this burden by having recourse to the arguments of his theory. Certainly, this burden on his conscience has as an element the fear of discovery. But, in spite of that, two levels are clearly exhibited: the one of his immediate value-grasping, of the voice of his conscience; the other, the theoretical level, on which he considers the voice of his conscience to be a mere fruit of silly conventions and traditions.

Thus we cannot compare his value blindness with regard

to murder with his deep understanding of purity and other moral values. The first is on the theoretical level, the other in the existential, immediate experience.

But at the bottom of the theory which blinds Raskolnikov, we also find a love for extra-moral personal values as embodied in the great, efficient personality, the man strong enough to pursue great and important aims without being thwarted and hindered by convention, public opinion, or custom.

It is in the light of this extra-moral value that Raskolnikov views the destruction of a wicked and mean old woman, whose ways are only a nuisance, nay, an evil, for society.

We are stressing the role of extra-moral values in the case of Raskolnikov, because the extra-moral, personal values in general play a great role in the origin of moral value blindness. In many cases, partial moral value blindness on the existential level of immediate experience is deeply connected with the emphasis laid on an extra-moral value. This over-emphasis, undoubtedly, is also rooted ultimately in pride and concupiscence. Yet the action of pride and concupiscence is a more indirect and subtle one than in the case in which certain moral values are not understood, because concupiscence bars insight into them. The worship of efficiency, of energy, or of a great and powerful personality darkens the awareness of certain moral disvalues, for instance, harshness, lack of meekness, lack of compassion, lack of warmth. Without the intervention of theories, the emphasis on such extra-moral, personal values overshadows certain moral values, whereas others are yet grasped. The worship of the natural, as opposed to the artificial and conventional, may sap the understanding of certain moral values, for instance, purity, faithfulness in marriage, humility; whereas these worshipers of extra-moral values grasp the value of reverence, justice, filial or parental devotion, solidarity in friendship, or veracity.

This type of value blindness, influenced by overemphasis on extra-moral values, is not necessarily in accordance with the objective difficulty of grasping a value because of its rank. According to the extra-moral value which is overemphasized, the moral value blindness will vary. If genuineness is the extra-moral value which is stressed, the moral values and disvalues ignored will not be the same as those overlooked when powerfulness, geniality, or energy is worshiped.

Summarizing, we may say that in the frame of partial moral value blindness due to the subconscious action of pride and concupiscence, we must distinguish three different types. First, the existential value blindness which is in accordance with the objective difficulty of understanding moral values. Secondly, a value blindness resulting from theories which act as a screen shutting out certain moral values. Here the value blindness may contradict the scale of objective difficulty in grasping moral values. Thirdly, the case in which overemphasis on extra-moral values perverts the "moral sense" and creates a blindness to certain moral values, a blindness which is independent of the objective rank of the moral values.

Our main concern will be this partial moral value blindness, the one resulting from overemphasis on extra-moral values.

Before turning to a more detailed analysis of this moral perversion, we must still deal briefly with the second main type of partial moral value blindness, which is due to tradition, education, and habit.

The moral authority of the parents has patently a great influence on the formation of the child's conscience. Whereas some moral values and disvalues, such as justice or injustice, are grasped intuitively at a very early age, and independently of any educational influence, other moral or morally relevant values and disvalues are thrown into relief by the command or prohibition of the parents. The categories of "commanded," "prohibited," and "permitted" undoubtedly play a large role in the child's conscience. Yet they in no way substitute for the perception of moral and morally relevant values. Not only are many moral and morally relevant values grasped independently of any command or prohibition, but even in the case in which a command or a prohibition paves the way for the knowledge of a moral or morally relevant value, the value perception is always something new with respect to the mere character of "commanded" and "prohibited." The "datum" of "commanded" and "prohibited" is present in cases in which no morally relevant value is at stake, as well as when a morally relevant value is in question.

To a child, a positive command by parents has, as such, a morally obliging character. To obey one's parents is, as such, morally good and even morally obligatory. But in growing up, the child grasps more and more the difference between a positive command of his parents and a moral commandment, i.e., something morally relevant intrinsically. Wrong as it is to try to reduce the datum of moral and morally relevant values and disvalues to the notion of "commanded or prohibited by a moral authority," there is no doubt that in presenting morally evil things to the child always as "permitted" or as morally unobjectionable, the grasping of the moral or morally relevant disvalue may be frustrated. Especially when the entire society in which a child is brought up considers certain things to be morally legitimate, a screen is placed before the morally relevant disvalue. Such seems to be the case with Mohammedan women who certainly do not grasp the immorality of polygamy. As above mentioned, polygamy is something taken for granted, which they know to be permitted by their religion and which they accept naïvely as morally unobjectionable. In this case we can hardly hold these women responsible for their partial moral value blindness. We cannot even say that their value blindness is determined by pride or concupiscence. True, there exists the possibility of piercing through this screen to the moral or morally relevant disvalue, despite an education and tradition in which it is regarded as morally unobjectionable or even as morally good. History discloses many cases in which outstanding moral personalities broke with their tradition and clearly grasped moral and morally relevant values and disvalues which were unknown to this tradition. But it remains doubtful whether we can make those persons responsible for remaining imprisoned in their tradition who, deformed by their education and tradition, are not strong enough as moral personalities to pierce through the screen erected by education and tradition.

Here further distinctions are necessary. First, the influence of education and tradition in silencing our conscience with respect to morally relevant disvalues is not independent of the question of which moral or morally relevant values are at stake. We mentioned already the scale of difficulty in grasping moral or morally relevant values. It has been stressed that, for instance, the immorality of polygamy is much more difficult to discover than the immorality of homicide or theft.

Thus, granted that in a Mohammedan woman it need not be pride or concupiscence which darkens her moral vision concerning polygamy, the same cannot be said of someone brought up in a tradition of pirates or of a tribe which considers the killing of aliens as morally legitimate. Certain moral or morally relevant disvalues are so evident and drastic that no education or tradition could possibly veil them if the person educated and living in this tradition were not himself caught to a great extent in the fangs of pride and concupiscence.

Insofar as these "evident" moral or morally relevant values are at stake, one must have a moral "weakness" and a low moral standard in order to let oneself be blinded by education and tradition.

Thus the fact of which moral or morally relevant disvalues are at stake, in a given case, plays a decisive role in the question whether or not tradition or education can "excuse" moral value blindness to such an extent that we may consider a person to be no longer responsible for his partial moral value blindness.[14]

It suffices to state that value blindness can be "excused" only in case of certain moral or morally relevant values or disvalues, and in those persons who grow up in a well-established tradition and who passively accept it, without actively embodying its ethics.

Therefore we mentioned only Mohammedan women, because they certainly accept polygamy as morally unobjectionable without embodying the ethos out of which this custom has grown. Mohammedan men, on the contrary, who profit from this custom, embody this ethos formed by concupiscence; and in them the fact is undeniable that an imprisonment in concupiscence, a yielding to concupiscence, goes hand in hand with their partial moral value blindness and nourishes this blindness.

This may suffice with respect to the partial moral value blindness due to education, tradition, and habit.

C. Formal Moral Value Blindness

We now turn to all those cases in which partial moral value blindness is due to pride or concupiscence. In this frame we concentrate on partial moral value blindness connected with an overemphasis on extra-moral values.

Here we have to distinguish the following different types of moral deformation. First, those who, without any hostile attitude toward the moral sphere, nevertheless fail to perceive the absolute primacy of the moral values with respect to all other values. We are thinking of people who grasp many moral and morally relevant values, without understanding their superiority with reference to extra-moral values. We could call this form of moral value blindness formal moral value blindness. Those who fall victim to it

---

[14] We prescind here from the difficult question whether such an "excuse" for partial moral value blindness can also be extended to those who *introduce* such a tradition, the "fathers" of a tradition.

will be unable to understand the superiority of a great moral personality, such as Socrates, to a brilliant statesman like Pericles or Caesar, or a great genius like Phidias or Sophocles. Extra-moral values seem to them equal or even superior.

Scheler made the distinction between four types of great men in the following hierarchical order: First, the saint; second, the genius; third, the hero; fourth, the inventor or technician.[15] In these four realms we find a hierarchical gradation, but the difference in rank between the different realms is such that the lowest in the realm of the saints surpasses the greatest of geniuses.[16] We quote Scheler's idea only in order to show the importance of the fact that one family of values, as such, ranks higher than another, without identifying ourselves with the details of Scheler's thesis.

Yet, as we have seen before, the moral sphere ranks higher than all other value domains. But more than that, it has a unique primacy, being the only one which belongs to the *unum necessarium*. To overlook its superiority and primacy is equivalent to overlooking an essential feature of every morally relevant and moral value. A man who fails to understand the incomparable superiority and absolute primacy of the moral sphere would still be under the cloud of a formal moral value blindness, even if he were to grasp all moral and morally relevant values, and were to grasp them as *values*.

This type is obviously only to be found among the morally unconscious type in the sense attributed to this term in *Christian Ethics*. Clearly not all morally unconscious people are necessarily affected by formal moral value blindness. But only morally unconscious people will possess it. They have a greater admiration for Napoleon or for Goethe than for a saint; they believe it to be more important that someone

15 Max Scheler. *Der Formalismus Kant's und die materiale Wertethik.* (Halle, Niemeyer, 1913.)

16 Regarding the saint, we must add that he surpasses the realm of natural values and implies thus a difference which is incomparable with all others: the one dividing the supernatural from the natural.

be a genius than an extraordinary personality from a moral point of view. They will also find that moral disvalues must be overlooked in a genius. Wrongly they apply to the moral sphere the words of Ovid: *"Quod licet Jovi non licet Bovi."* Their specific blindness refers thus to two formal features of the moral sphere: its incomparable superiority to all value domains and its indispensability.[17] They do not see that moral values rank higher than all other values, and that to be morally good is indispensable for every man, that it belongs to the "one thing which is necessary" for man; that no other value, intellectual or vital, great as it may be, can compensate for the absence of a moral value, and still less for the presence of a moral disvalue.

From this formal moral value blindness we must distinguish a much less serious moral deformation. We are thinking of persons for whom someone's intelligence, wit, or charm —all of which are extra-moral values—play a greater role in their sympathy and in the selection of their friends than moral standards. In principle they will admit that the moral question is much more important in itself and they will grant that moral values deserve more praise than others, but personally they will be more attracted by certain extra-moral values. Extra-moral values will be a more decisive measure for the heart, although reason may recognize the moral values as being the more decisive measure. There is a split between the moral conviction exhibited in their judgments and the immediate reaction in their hearts.

This deformation based on a split between the conviction (the attitude toward the moral sphere on principle) and the existential role of the extra-moral values is not a formal moral value blindness, but belongs to a completely different type of moral deformation, which can be found also among faithful Catholics. It concerns the question of how far the moral sphere has acquired its incontestable primacy in the

[17] *Christian Ethics*, Chapter 15.

practical existential order. Certainly it is due to pride and concupiscence when this moral sphere does not play the role it should in the life and heart of a man. Two marks are characteristic of this deformation. First, the fact that it is not the conflict between the subjectively satisfying and the moral sphere (a conflict existing for every man), but the conflict between extra-moral values on the one hand, and the moral and morally relevant values on the other.

Secondly, the conflict is not experienced as a problem. It is not one of the many cases in which our conviction is overrun by a tendency of our nature, or in which we fail to correspond with our love and joy, admiration and enthusiasm, to the call of the values. Such is the ever-recurring situation of all men, even if they have the ardent will to be morally good and to conform to the call of the morally relevant values, and to correspond with their hearts to the objective hierarchy of values. But in the case we are now discussing the striking feature is this, that the inadequacy is not even experienced as an evil, and thus there is no striving for a change in this respect. It is a kind of imperfection of its own which could be called a moral lack of wakefulness.

### D. The Specific Deformations Embodied in the Substitute

A radically different deformation of morality is at stake in the case in which an extra-moral value assumes the character of a *substitute* for morality, in which it is introduced as the general denominator and norm in the realm of the morally good and evil. There are many things which can assume the role of a substitute morality, such as tradition, the laws of state, and honor, found as moral code in certain societies and cultural epochs, as well as in individuals. The value blindness here in question is again a completely different one. In contradistinction to the above-mentioned formal moral value blindness, here the primacy and indispensability of the moral sphere are understood and admitted. But the qualitative content of morality is deformed and perverted through an extra-moral value or an extra-moral aspect, or an extra-moral measure which assumes the role of a denominator of morality.

This qualitative falsification of morality is not necessarily present in the first type who places extra-moral values above moral values. This type of man leaves, as it were, the moral values qualitatively intact, but still prefers extra-moral values to these genuine moral values. He considers extraordinary intellectual and artistic gifts as ranking higher than charity, justice, veracity, purity. And by that he patently misunderstands and overlooks the general formal character of moral values.

But here in the substitutes, it is a qualitative falsification of the moral sphere. The compromise with pride and concupiscence displays itself not in overlooking the formal primacy of morality, but in an interpretation of the moral sphere which does not force pride and concupiscence to abdicate completely. The wrong general denominator will, more or less, exclude many moral values from the moral sphere and thus restrict the morally relevant values, while simultaneously including goods as morally relevant which are in reality morally irrelevant. But this restriction concerns the content and not the formal role of the moral sphere. To this falsified moral sphere a great role may be assigned. Though the moral sphere is qualitatively deformed, the formal primacy and indispensability of morality are not denied. It is certainly affected by the substitute, for it has no longer the true primacy and indispensability, but its most formal character is preserved. The question arises: Are these substitutes—such as the above-mentioned formal moral blindness—to be found only among morally unconscious people?

In the frame of moral consciousness, in the sense attributed to this term in *Christian Ethics*, substitutes for morality have no place. The morally conscious man, with his general will to be good and his awareness of his vocation to sanction and disavow, possesses an understanding of the moral sphere which excludes all deformations of morality and compromises with pride and concupiscence, and leaves room only for an open war with pride and concupiscence.[18]

We mentioned in *Christian Ethics* that even in the case of morally unconscious men, different forms of a spurious general will to be morally good can be found.[19]

We also saw that we can no longer speak of moral unconsciousness in the case of the morally evil men who are dominated by pride. But we saw that they are just the opposite of the morally conscious man. Now we have to analyze the type of consciousness which is proper to many adherents of a substitute morality. The man who considers the moral question to be the most important one, and strives to live according to the moral norm as he conceives it, but whose moral norm is a substitute for the true moral norm, implying a compromise with pride and concupiscence, is not necessarily a morally unconscious type, but still less a morally conscious type in our sense of the term.

The fundamental difference between the adherent of a substitute morality and the man who strives to follow the true natural moral law, from the point of view of moral consciousness, consists in this: the substitute morality embodies a subconscious compromise between the moral value-responding center on the one hand, and pride and concupiscence on the other.

This compromise is accomplished in a deep stratum. In substituting an extra-moral value or measure for the moral norm, pride or concupiscence is "spared." Because it is falsified, the moral sphere becomes acceptable to a mitigated

18 This, however, does not imply that the morally conscious man is safeguarded against self-delusions.

19 "It is not the free attitude of the morally conscious. It is more a general antipathy to immorality, a half-conscious desire to abstain from moral evil.... When asked why he acted in this way on a certain occasion, this morally unconscious type will answer, 'Because I dislike being mean or bad.'" *Christian Ethics*, pp. 266-267.

pride and concupiscence. But such a compromise contradicts precisely the very nature of moral consciousness.

For moral consciousness, in our sense, the unconditioned *will to submit* to the moral commandments is essential, an attitude which strictly contradicts the adhering to substitutes. Even if he who adheres to a substitute has the general, superactual will to live in conformity with it, this willing essentially differs from the superactual will to submit to the true moral law, to be morally good in the authentic and true sense of moral goodness. The will to live in conformity with the substitute is restricted and conditioned by the underlying compromise, even if it has a radical and iron character. If the man who has identified morally good and evil with honorable and dishonorable, and has substituted his honor for the moral norm, watches anxiously his honor and is even willing to sacrifice his life rather than be dishonorable, the ardor for this substitute, the determined conscious will to conform to this measure, is nevertheless restricted and limited from the moral point of view. First, the very fact that an extra-moral value or measure substitutes for the true moral norm excludes the true unlimitedness of submission. The substitute, as it were, provides for the restriction and limitation of a surrender to the true moral law, and ultimately to God.

Secondly, the zeal with which one obeys the norm of the substitute is an impure one from the moral point of view; it is fed and supported by the appeal which this substitute makes to pride and concupiscence. It has, thus, an extra-moral strength and *not* a moral one; in many cases it even includes elements of an evil zeal.

Moral consciousness presupposes the confrontation with true morality, with the unique challenge which only true moral values possess, and implies the awareness of this unique challenge as well as the pure value-responding will to submit to this challenge. It is thus clearly incompatible with any substitute for morality.

The difference between moral consciousness and the kind of consciousness which tolerates substitutes for morality manifests itself also with respect to sanction and disavowal. The moral consciousness, as we have shown in *Christian Ethics,* is characterized by the awareness of our power of sanction and disavowal and of the fact that the morally relevant values and the moral norm call for sanctioning and disavowal. But we do not find such awareness in the adherent of a substitute morality. We discussed, in *Christian Ethics,* several forms of pseudo-sanctioning, of an express identification of ourselves with an affective response arising spontaneously in our soul.[20] In an analogous way, we find that in the adherent of honor a kind of disavowal may take place with respect to affective responses. He may disavow his fear, because he considers it to be dishonorable; he may disavow his compassion or any feeling of insecurity in the presence of another. But this disavowal clearly differs from the true one in the morally conscious man. This disavowal lacks the capacity of invalidating an affective response, which we find in the disavowal of the morally conscious man. In this disavowal one does not break through to a higher level; it lacks the character of acquiring moral freedom. As we saw in *Christian Ethics,* the true moral disavowal can only flow out of the response to the moral sphere. It implies necessarily a concerting with the logos of true morality. The same applies to the man for whom the laws of the state are substituted for morality as to the adherent of honor.

We must also distinguish the adherent to a substitute morality from the morally unconscious man such as we have described him in *Christian Ethics,* or such as Tom Jones in the novel of Fielding, or *l'ingénu,* in Voltaire's novel of the same name. The man who identifies the moral law with the law of the state may consciously strive to live up to this moral ideal of correctness, the ideal of a decent citizen. He

[20] *Christian Ethics,* p. 326 ff.

may in no way simply follow the inclinations of his nature, he may even struggle against all tendencies which would imply a conflict with the law of the state.[21]

The difference between this adherent of a substitute for morality and the morally unconscious man consists not in the fact that a struggle of the will against a natural inclination may be found in the one, but not in the other. Such a struggle is also possible in the morally unconscious man. But the fact of a conscious striving to conform to a norm, which presents itself as imperative and possesses the most formal features of morality, is the decisive difference. The man for whom honor or loyalty to the state, or tradition or self-control, is the standard of morality may anxiously confront everything with this standard. He thus obviously lacks the ingenuity, the naïvety, of the morally unconscious man.

A former type of Prussian officer who lived by the sword of "honor," and confronted everything with it, had a moral denominator which is not to be found in the morally uncon-

---

[21] A conscious struggling with his will against a desire, an inclination of his nature, is clearly also to be found in the morally unconscious man. Insofar as he grasps moral values, it may happen that he overcomes with his will tendencies of his nature which contradict these moral values.

We have to realize that struggling against the tendencies of our nature is frequent in the extra-moral sphere and even among certain types of criminals or radically evil persons. The evil man who overcomes his fear, in order to attain his evil goal, or who suppresses his compassion, is well known. How often one suppresses his love because of financial interests or because of certain class prejudices; how often one does violence to his nature in order to make a good impression on other people, especially if he wants to obtain something from them.

Thus, the struggle against a natural tendency, as such, is in no way a sign of moral consciousness; it occurs even among morally unconscious men. It is only when we consider the nature of this struggle that the difference to the morally conscious man stands forth. The "reason" for this struggle here is also something which a man's nature invites him to do—it is either some extra-moral interest which is stronger than the tendency against which he fights, or some value response to which his nature invites him—but he never reaches in this struggle the inner "distance" to his nature, as it happens to be, this free acting against it, which is only possible as a response to the true moral sphere.

scious type. The morally unconscious type has no definite principles; led by his inclination, he lives rather spontaneously in relation to the good or bad. The adherent of substitutes, on the contrary, may have "principles"; his life may have the purposiveness, conscious framework, order which are alien to the morally unconscious type.

Yet we do not intend to say by this that this kind of consciousness is to be found in every man whose conception of the moral sphere is blurred or distorted by a substitute. There are many morally unconscious people who, because of their life in a community in which an extra-moral value or measure substitutes for the moral law and the moral norm, move and live in the frame of these substitutes. They will not be preoccupied with this pseudo-norm; they will not strive to live up to this norm, but will rather follow the bent of their nature, responding only to those values which appeal to them. Nevertheless, they may be influenced by the substitutes of the society in which they live, so that whatever conception they have of the moral sphere will betray this influence.

But they will not be conscious ardent adherents of substitute morality; they will never be men of "principles." Certainly never "zealots" or "moralists." Thus we have to state as follows: The deformation of the moral sphere by a substitute may be found among morally unconscious men as well as among those who are not morally unconscious. But the typical, active adherent of a substitute morality is not a morally unconscious type. It is this moral semi-consciousness or, as we may call it, this "conscious-unconsciousness" which is characteristic of the typical adherent of a substitute. He is a man who has moral principles, who has a critical attitude toward his nature, who lives and judges according to a norm. But he differs from the morally conscious type. Moral consciousness in our sense implies an awakening to the true moral sphere, a confrontation with the unique challenge of the moral sphere. The adherent of a substitute morality is typically "imprisoned" in himself; he lives in this intra-human space, incapable of emerging to the awareness of man's metaphysical situation. If we compare the Assyrians or the Phoenicians to the Greeks, we observe emerging from the intellect of the Greeks a unique sense of "distance" to the world and to objects, a disentanglement from the pragmatic absorption which imprisons man, as it were, among the things surrounding him. The sense of distance of the *homo sapiens* among the Greeks, this "clear eye" looking wonderingly into the world instead of taking everything for granted, made the Greeks the real fathers of philosophical knowledge. While the awakening of the Greeks has a certain analogy to the moral awakening proper to true moral consciousness, the attitude of these other peoples (Assyrians or Phoenicians) has some analogy to the semi-consciousness of the adherent of a substitute morality.

Having distinguished the semi-consciousness of the typical adherent of a substitute morality from true moral consciousness, we can continue with our analysis of the moral substitute.

The striking feature of this perversion of the moral sphere is that not only is a partial moral blindness connected with the overemphasis on an extra-moral value, but an extra-moral value sets itself up as the representative of the entire moral sphere. Although in reality an extra-moral value, it is garbed in certain formal features of the moral sphere.

Here there is not only a restriction in the vision of moral and morally relevant values, a restriction which always affects the entire ethos, not only an incompleteness of moral value perception, under the influence of an extra-moral value; but the extra-moral value arrogates to itself the place of morality, is disguised as a moral norm and identified with the moral sphere. Thus there results a mixture of its material extra-moral quality and of the most formal features of the moral sphere and theme.

Yet in saying that this extra-moral value in moral guise

has received formulation, we do not mean that such formulation is the result of a theory and exists only on a merely theoretical level. One must distinguish the deformations resulting from a wrong philosophy, or from pre-philosophical reasoning, from the existential deformations. By the "formulated" substitute, we mean an existential lived ideal which has received formulation as a norm only because it has reached a certain degree of consciousness.

In stressing its formulated character, we want to oppose this substitute for morality to the partial moral value blindness resulting from an overemphasis on an extra-moral value which, however, does not attain the character of a formal representative of the moral sphere. We could call this partial moral value blindness naïve and accidental; whereas, in the case of the substitutes, it is more conscious, and sustained by principles. Both are existential, situated on the level of experience, and not a superimposed product of theorizing. But the partial moral blindness here described is a deformation which manifests itself in the deficient grasping of some moral or morally relevant values, and in a corresponding perversion of the entire ethos. The substitute, on the contrary, is a conscious moral norm, not necessarily formulated theoretically and rarely substructured by a philosophical theory, but still formulated as a notion.

We mentioned above that the "mediocre" man who wants to serve two masters, God and mammon, as described in *Christian Ethics,* is but one of the several types of compromise between the "reverent, loving, humble center" on the one hand, and pride and concupiscence on the other hand. All the different forms of partial moral value blindness due to the influence of pride and concupiscence involve a compromise. The compromise is not necessarily accomplished consciously, and it must not manifest itself in an ethos proper to a mediocre man, who shuns every risk and every full abandonment. The compromise proper to all the other different forms of value blindness takes place in a deeper, less conscious stratum. To a certain extent the person lets himself be dominated by pride and concupiscence. He yields to pride and concupiscence, and fails to wage a conscious and decisive war against them. He has not the unconditioned will to be morally good, which is ready to struggle against his pride and concupiscence. Because of this compromise in the very depth of his personality, he is blind to certain moral values. But there is no ethos involved here, an ethos characterized by the "non-commitment" of mediocre cowardice and the desire to avoid getting into trouble.

What has just been said concerning partial moral value blindness also applies to the different substitutes for morality. The man who identifies morally good and evil with honorable and dishonorable may be a fanatic in his ethos and ready to make every sacrifice when his honor is at stake. He may be radically opposed in his ethos to the mediocre man, he may be far from shunning a full and unconditioned response. But his moral norm, his substitute for morality, is patently the result of a compromise. Although the compromise here implies no ethos of "non-commitment," the fact that an extra-moral value interwoven with moral elements holds the place of the true morally good and evil is, as such, a clear manifestation of a compromise between the morally good center and pride or concupiscence.

The perversion of morality which the substitute embodies is a clear compromise because the substitute does take into account the requests of pride or concupiscence, and simultaneously includes an undeniable link to the moral sphere, i.e., an element of response to the moral sphere, the acknowledgment of a norm which calls for obedience, which is above and independent of one's subjective desires and wishes.

This twofold aspect of the substitute clearly betrays the misalliance out of which it was born: the combination of extra-moral elements with the most general features of the formal moral sphere and the moral theme. All substitutes, though in a very different degree, imply a perversion of the moral sphere, but still preserve the most general formal character of this sphere. Or, as we may express it, the adherents of a substitute morality have made many subconscious concessions to pride and to concupiscence, but they are still linked in one way or another to the moral sphere.

The extra-moral elements which substitute for morality are either extra-moral values, extra-moral goods and norms, or extra-moral aspects of certain moral values. In order to understand the specific nature of the substitutes, we must analyze the nature of extra-moral values and goods which play a role in the substitutes, as well as inquire why they are more readily acceptable to pride and concupiscence as norms than the true moral and morally relevant values, or the true natural moral law. We must further examine the extra-moral aspects of certain moral and morally relevant values and ask why they are attractive to pride or concupiscence.

Yet, before we turn to this fundamental task, we must still make some distinctions concerning the range of the role of the substitutes and later on offer a brief enumeration of the main types of substitutes.

## E. Degrees of Deformation

We must still distinguish several distortions of morality which are more or less akin to the substitutes. The difference between the substitute in the proper sense of the word and these deformations lies in the way in which certain specific values and norms arrogate to themselves an illegitimate role in morality.

The substitute in the full sense—either a formal notion or a specific value (moral or extra-moral) —is identified with the general denominator of morality: moral goodness.

This identification does not take the form of a thesis— of a theoretical equation—but is rather one which is accomplished existentially and without philosophical reflection.

This is the most radical form of substitution. From this

we must distinguish the case in which a specific value (moral or extra-moral) is not identified with the sphere of morally good and evil, but forms nevertheless the bulk of morality, the decisive measure in questions of moral judgments. Let us think of the "errant knight" for whom honor was the great and decisive point, although he recognized that there were moral values and moral disvalues outside the realm of the honorable and the dishonorable. Yet his great concern was the norm of honor.

Here a specific value or idea is the one thing to which one should conform above all. What is incompatible with it should above all be shunned and avoided. The specific norm is not made into the general denominator of morality (as in the typical substitute). The specific norm here is only considered to be the *core* of morality, the part of morality which is taken with full seriousness, and which overshadows all else, which is nonetheless acknowledged.

In this perversion one yields to a specific value the role of the core of morality. The result of this perversion is not a substitute for morality, but an alleged core of morality.

In this case also we are confronted with a perversion of morality, although it is a less radical one than in the case of the real substitute. It entails, first, a wrong title under which many morally evil things are condemned; secondly, a wrong hierarchy among the morally relevant values, as a result of making a specific value the core of morality; thirdly, an extra-moral point of view which plays a predominant role and invades the moral sphere.

From the substitutes and the alleged cores of morality, we must distinguish a third degree of the illegitimate role of certain moral or extra-moral values, namely, when values form a kind of ideal image which a person—consciously or subconsciously—has set for himself. Though he will admit that there exist other moral values which are just as obligatory, he will consider living by this image much more important than conforming to the other moral values.

One man, for instance, will make it his ideal to be "reasonable" and to avoid everything which is foolish; another, to be "noble" and thus to avoid above all anything mean. Both will in no way claim that these moral values are the only ones. On the contrary, they will not only admit that there are many other moral values, but even that they may rank as high as the ones which form their "moral" image. But they have no other care than to live up to this moral image; and they will tolerate any faults of their own so long as they do not specifically contradict this moral image.

This illegitimate function of specific moral values clearly differs much from the two above-mentioned perversions: the substitute and the alleged core of morality. "Reasonability" or "nobility" are neither considered as coextensive with morality, nor are they considered to be the objectively most important part of morality. But the individual we are considering has made them his own personal ideal, a hidden ideal which he aspires to fulfill; and in discovering moral disvalues in himself which contradict this ideal, he is more despondent and more eager to overcome them than when he discovers other moral disvalues which do not specifically contradict this ideal. There will be a greater readiness to admit faults so long as they do not touch this ideal. He will even be very indulgent toward them, although he will not deny that they are regrettable and that they should be overcome.

Such a person does not feel really tainted by them; he is not repulsive to himself because of these faults; but he will be much less willing to admit as faults whatever in his opinion contaminates this immanent moral ideal.

And when he can no longer really deny to himself that he has failed to live up to this ideal, he is much more depressed; he is seriously disturbed, and hates himself for not having lived up to it. He feels deeply ashamed.

The perversion here has a character thoroughly different from the two former ones. Yet it also introduces an extra-moral aspect into the moral sphere. This subjective moral ideal draws its attractiveness from an extra-moral aspect of certain moral values.[22] The ideal of "nobleness" has an aesthetic connotation: meanness is something specifically ugly. The ideal of "reasonability" has also the connotation of an extra-moral value. And it is only because of these extra-moral aspects that they are subjectively preferred. If they were grasped only under the aspect of their moral value, they would not be granted a privileged status; their role would be seen as corresponding to their objective rank.

The role of such extra-moral aspects in the moral life of a man is an obvious contamination of the basic moral attitude. To allow an extra-moral value to matter so much so that it overrules the purely moral point of view, while dividing the sphere of moral disvalues into one part which we want above all to avoid, and another which we tolerate to a degree, is indisputably a perversion. Moreover, it weakens our moral striving against all moral faults which do not directly contradict the moral ideal of ourselves.

We shall concentrate mainly on the *substitutes,* that is to say, on those formal notions or material values which are taken as substitute for the entire moral sphere, and partly on those which at least illegitimately claim to be the most serious part of morality: the alleged cores of morality. The distortion produced by the subjective hidden ideals belongs more to the problem of the role of extra-moral motivations in our moral life.

[22] Cf. Chapter VII.

CHAPTER III

# SURVEY OF THE MAIN SUBSTITUTES

IT IS NOT OUR intention to inquire into the question how many types of substitutes for morality there exist. The list of substitutes which we offer here does not claim to be complete. It is restricted to the main substitutes and is concerned more with mentioning different types of substitutes than with a complete enumeration of all substitutes which belong to one type or another.

We already mentioned some of them in the course of our analysis of the nature of the substitute as such. We shall mention them again now in our survey of the main types of substitutes.

There exist two main types of substitutes: the formal substitute and the material or qualitative substitute. We begin here with the formal substitute.

First, we find persons, tribes, and communities which identify the moral law with tradition. The measure for good and evil is conformity or non-conformity with tradition. The norm for determining whether something is morally commanded, permitted, or prohibited, is tradition.

Again, we find persons for whom the moral sphere is identical with the laws of the state in which they live. Morality is identified with loyalty to the state. The authority of the state has taken the place of the authority of the moral law. The borders of morality are circumscribed by that which the law of a state prohibits, permits, or commands. A man of this type is horrified by the idea that he could be disloyal, that he could transgress a law of the state. But moral disvalues which are not embraced within the laws of the state, and

39

especially those which by their very nature are beyond the range of state laws, are overlooked, i.e., their immorality is not understood. Patently, there is a great variety of shades within the frame of this type, ranging from a naïve loyalty to a bourgeois correctness.

Another formal substitute is progressiveness or liberalism. Moral goodness is identified with broad-mindedness, desire of progress, tolerance. Several fundamental moral values such as purity, reverence, humility are not included in morality. Other moral values such as justice, veracity, generosity are seen in the light of the open-minded liberalism, erroneously interpreted as consequences of this mentality.

This formal substitute has already a more constant quality than the identification of morality with tradition or state laws. The moral question culminates for adherents of this substitute in progressiveness or liberalism; and the word "reactionary" is for them the very epitome of all moral repulsiveness.[1]

In turning to the main material or qualitative substitutes we find, first, the man who identifies morally good and evil with honorable and dishonorable. For this man *honor* has become the moral norm. What honor forbids, what is incompatible with his honor, he wants to avoid, to abstain from. The sphere of morality is here circumscribed by honor. This substitute is widespread. Honor as a measure plays a large role, not only as substitute, but also as the core of morality, as its most serious part.

For other people morality is identical with humaneness, with warmth of heart; and any law which imposes a control on the spontaneous impulses of our heart is seen as the expression of a monstrous rigidity, a bureaucratic pharisaism. This ethos is especially to be found among Slavic people. In Tolstoianism, we find features of it, and it is often the

---

[1] A special case is the man who recognizes but one real value: democracy. But this is more on the theoretical level. In reality this man will also include veracity, reliability, and loyalty as true values.

morality to which the so-called "bohemian" adheres. Every rule, every precept is seen as something inhuman, cool, heartless and, moreover, conventional and artificial. Even reason is suspect for such people. Thus morally good is iden-tified with spontaneity, warm unconventionality, the posses-sion of a sensitive overflowing heart. What is morally evil tends to be identified with loyalty to juridical obligations, correctness, bureaucratism, or cool reasonability. The bour-geois is for those people the embodiment of moral disvalues, the very antithesis of the unconventional humane "bohe-mian" who embodies their moral ideal.

Another substitute for morality is to be found in those who identify morality with duty, interpreted as the fulfillment of a clearly circumscribed task, preferably a task which is acces-sible to juridical notions. The adherent of this substitute will recognize the moral obligation of doing what he promised to do, or of helping a relative, but he will never admit any obligation to help anybody to whom he is not related.[2] Com-passion, charity, generosity have no place in this morality. Duty is understood as the reliable, correct fulfillment of any "tasks" familiar, professional, religious; and the circumfer-ence of morality coincides with the fulfillment of these "duties." The morally evil man is here equivalent with the unreliable one, who fails to do his duty, in this sense of the term: the scamp.

Related to this substitute is also the identification of morality with faithfulness, i.e., faithfulness to our friends, faithfulness to our country, faithfulness to our profession, to our superiors. This faithfulness is a specific mixture of loyalty, reliability, sincerity, frankness, solidarity, devotion. Moreover, it adds to the correctness of "duty" a still more qualitative element of true-heartedness, a note of the heart which the "duty" norm did not include. The famous *Nibe-lungentreue* so often claimed by the Germans to be their

2 Cf. *True Morality and Its Counterfeits,* Chapter 5.

special virtue, in contradistinction to the "slyness" of the Italians, more concerned with their personal advantage, is a typical example of this substitute. The naïve man who trusts, who presupposes all people to be veracious because of his own true-heartedness, who is the prey of sly and shrewd people, who does not quit his post, even when all the others have abandoned it, the man on whose word and devotion one can unconditionally rely, represents the ideal of moral goodness, which is here the substitute morality.

A widespread substitute for morality is altruism. Often moral goodness is identified with service to others. The only moral measure is whether something is "egoistic" or "altruistic." To desire happiness is considered "immoral," even longing for noble goods endowed with high values is believed to be egoistic. Every striving for our own perfection is "selfish." Morality consists exclusively in being absorbed in the service of others, The adherents of this substitute look with indignation at anyone who does not consider himself a mere instrument in the service of other persons. They have an ethos which is a peculiar mixture of devotion and indignation.

Sometimes this altruism assumes the specific note of "social sense" expressing itself in a preoccupation with social justice. Moral goodness is identified with social sense; moral badness with the lack of social sense. Whether someone is pure, humble, or meek matters not. The only thing which counts is his sense for social welfare and social institutions, his striving for social improvement, his devotion and efficiency in this respect. The evil man, par excellence, is the man who takes no interest in social improvements—the conservative. And even great artists are considered to be egoists insofar as they dedicate their lives to "cultural" things, to a domain which is considered more or less superfluous luxury, something for the upper four hundred.

This humanitarian substitute is specifically interesting because, seemingly, it is only an illegitimate curtailing of the moral sphere. Yet in truth it is not only a one-sidedness, but a falsification of the moral sphere, as a mere substitute for morality. Only it is one of those substitutes in which a special moral value—not an extra-moral one—is identified with morality, as such. Hence the deformation of morality which is to be found in every substitute is fully present in this case.

Again, we find people who identify morality with self-control. The good man is the one who can control himself; who possesses self-dominion, strength of will, and energy; who is his own master. The "immoral," despicable man is the one who is a prey to his passions and emotions, who is ruled by events and by the situations in which he is placed instead of remaining aloof.

This substitute is typical, not only for Stoic ethics, but for the innumerable existential Stoic types which we find throughout history. This substitute is often linked with an idol of self-containment. Self-esteem, respect for one's own dignity, is here the core of morality. To shed tears is believed to be despicable; to lose one's temper, to lose one's head is the epitome of immorality; to get drunk is for the adherents of this ideal worse than to be hardhearted, uncharitable, or avaricious.[8]

Another well-known substitute is the ideal of the "never too much" or cheap reasonability in the sense of a moderation which abstains from any intensity and thus from heroic abandonment, filing them under the title of "exaggerations." It is the specific substitute of the mediocre man. Here the compromise which—as we saw—is typical of every substitute is also reflected in the mediocre man's ethos. Morality is identified with this shoddy reasonability, immorality with "unreasonableness." Reasonability has here the same meaning as in the term "marriage of reason." Instead of the true

[8] This substitute of virile dignity must be clearly distinguished from the extra-moral or even anti-moral idols of virility. For many, "wrath," losing one's temper in a "hard" way, as well as getting drunk, is a sign of virility.

reasonability which requires that we always conform to the theme in question, "reasonability" in the case of a "marriage of reason" means casting aside love—the true motive of marriage—and therefore acting "unreasonably" in the true and high sense of this term. "Reasonable" acquires here the sense of being a so-called "realist," of admitting as objective and important only such factors which can be coolly grasped at a distance and calculated. This mediocre reasonability regards all heroism as an unhealthy exaltation; every risk a temerarious adventure; every full self-donation, even every unconditioned value response, a despicable recklessness.

Another widespread substitute which is, in some respects, akin to this morality of "moderation" is the so-called *bien pensant*, the decent man, whom society respects as opposed to every "disordered" type, whether a bohemian, a beggar, or a revolutionary.

In this typical "bourgeois" substitute, morality is identified with a mixture of certain real moral values (such as reliability, honesty, and loyalty) and with conventional elements (such as conformity with the rules of society). The moral man is one who behaves in a way that society considers respectable. Even belonging to a "good family" is an element of respectability whereby the "goodness" may refer to wealth, social standard, aristocratic origin, and so on.

In this substitute, the "decent" man is opposed to the "indecent one," with whom one cannot shake hands, because he has scandalized society, either having once been imprisoned, or having had his name in the newspapers in an unfavorable context. How many real moral virtues are included in this decency may greatly vary according to the type of society. But in all cases it is a mere substitute, a distortion of morality, and never covers all moral values, apart from having some conventional bourgeois taint. It always implies a mixture of extra-moral conventional elements and moral values; yet not only a mixture but, what is worse, a confusion of both. Moral goodness, i.e., moral decency, is looked upon as the privilege of a class, sometimes even of a political party: on the one hand, there are the morally decent people, reliable, clean, honest, correct; and on the other, the morally indecent, "impossible" people—outcasts, pariahs, the scum of society.

Another widespread substitute for morality is the ideal of the gentleman. It is partly akin to honor, partly to the *bien pensant*. Yet in contradistinction to both, there is an aesthetic element, a certain moral elegance and graciousness which honor does not necessarily possess, and which the notion of *bien pensant* certainly does not include.

This norm may again greatly vary in its qualitative content. Sometimes, the gentleman is conceived as the man who is not only reliable but generous, veracious, honest, noble, distinguished, sensitive. And one contrasts him with the coarse, mean, unreliable dishonest man, the scamp. Sometimes the notion of gentleman may sink to a much lower level. The main stress may be laid on good manners, politeness, society standard; but even then it will include always certain moral virtues, such as reliability, to be true to one's promises, fairness.

It always will possess this aesthetic value of gentleness which is not implied in the *bien pensant*. This gentleness also may not be present in many ideals of honor, for instance, the rigid, stiff honor of the Prussian officer. To identify moral goodness with gentlemanliness, or at least to make it the core of moral worthiness, is a specific Anglo-Saxon feature (at least in later modern times).

We have discussed previously various stages of the role of an extra-moral value or norm. We distinguished there between substitutes in the strict sense and the alleged core of morality. All the norms just enumerated can function as substitutes for morality, as well as alleged cores of morality.

Other norms, however, can only have the function of representing the "bulk" or core of morality, and are never complete substitutes for morality. We shall now briefly enumerate the main specimens of this latter kind.

There are, first, people who consider efficiency to be the center of morality. They will admit that there exist also other moral virtues; they will not deny, for instance, that generosity or moral courage is praiseworthy. But for them the main moral question is: Is this man efficient, i.e., assiduous, reliable, energetic, or is he a helpless prey to his paralyzing inhibitions,[4] his laziness, his timorousness? This will be the measure which they apply in their judgment of other persons and of themselves. It will function as the prism for their moral evaluation. They will say: "This man is not worth anything; one cannot count upon him; one cannot deal with him; he is completely inefficient." And if one objects that this man has, nevertheless, positive moral qualities, that he is, for instance, meek and charitable, humble and generous, they will answer with a condescendent smile: "Yes, we do not deny that he may also have some good qualities, but he is an 'impossible' man, he cannot be taken seriously as a moral personality; he is a 'good for nothing.' " They may pity him, but will despise him, nonetheless.

Another type of norm which claims to represent the core of morality is duty, in the sense of what is hard for us, that which contradicts the inclinations and tendencies of our heart. It is a widespread rigorist conception of morality. Certainly other moral values will also be admitted, but the part of morality which is really admired, which really counts, begins with the things which are enforced on our heart, on our natural tendencies, and which cost us sweat and tears. The danger of making hardship a measure of moral merit is so widespread that even a genius like Bergson is not free from it, as is shown by his words: "The moral rule which

[4] Let us think of a man like Oblomov, in Goncharov's novel of the same name.

appears to me the highest and most truthful is to choose of two duties the one that costs the more." [5]

Again we find people for whom the center of morality consists in being "genuine," true to oneself,[6] as opposed to all kinds of mannerisms, affectation, ungenuineness, pose, insincerity, falseness. They will not deny that justice, honesty, warmth of heart are moral values, and praiseworthy. But the norm by which they primarily judge others and themselves is whether someone is genuine or not. They may say: It is true this man is a prey to his passions, he is not a model of purity, but, after all, he is true to himself, he is sincere and genuine, he is no hypocrite, he does not try to give an impression of himself other than of what he really is, he is not affected, is no boaster, no phony, no sham; he is true to his nature.

The perversion which the overemphasis of this misinterpreted moral value entails is easy to grasp. Not only does it darken the true hierarchy of moral values, but it deforms the ethos and falsifies the entire morality. The people who adhere to this norm tend to see even every moral effort as savoring insincerity and mere exaltation. Every moral *élan* is accepted with suspicion, as an ungenuine expression of the person's nature. The more immediate and impulsive a manifestation of an inner attitude is, the more it is believed to be true and genuine. Often we find also an ideal of false "chastity" in these people; they feel a kind of shame at the very idea of striving for moral perfection, as if this would already be a pretentious pharisaism. To show enthusiasm for a virtue which one does not possess appears to them already to be untrue, ungenuine, in some way unchaste. Judgments, words, expressions of all kinds should never disagree with our nature, with our character as it actually is. Understatements are regarded as the

---

[5] Floris Delattre, "Les Dernières Années d'Henri Bergson," *Revue Philosophique*, Nos. 3, 8, March, August 1941, p. 138.

[6] Thérèse Desqueyroux, Maurois.

symptom of this genuineness and chastity; overstatements as the peak of a despicable ungenuineness.

Again we find people for whom courage is the core of morality. The main question is: Is this person a courageous man or a coward? Courage above all deserves esteem; the worst blame, for these people, is to be called timorous, or a coward. They will pardon many other moral faults if only a man has courage.

Clearly, it is not moral courage which is here considered as the pattern of morality. It is physical as well as' psychical courage, either as a temperamental disposition or as the result of a strong will.[7] Certainly moral courage is also included, but the fundamental difference between moral and extra-moral courage is not grasped, and moral courage is erroneously seen as a species of extra-moral courage. This overemphasis of courage is mostly connected with a virility idol. What matters is to be a man, not a child, not a woman; and in praising courageous women, these people will say: They are like men. Courage is regarded as the core of moral seriousness, of reliability, of the capacity to cope with life and all its vicissitudes. It is that which before all else elicits admiration.

Again in some people, it is a specific *moral* value which assumes illegitimately the role of the core of morality, for instance, nobleness as opposed to meanness. These people will not deny that there exist also other moral values and disvalues, but they will assure us that they perhaps may do wrong, but never will they do something base. To avoid

[7] We shall discuss the difference between moral and extra-moral courage *in extenso* in Chapter V. Here it may suffice to say that in moral courage we do not shrink from facing a danger if it is unavoidable in order to conform to a call of a morally relevant good. The man who risks his life in order to save his neighbor manifests moral courage. Extra-moral courage refers to our attitude toward dangers, physical or non-physical, when no morally relevant good is in question. Climbing Mount Everest exemplifies extra-moral courage.

what is vile seems to them the really important moral obligation. They will also, in judging other persons, question
whether or not their actions are base. The specifically ugly,
ill-smelling character of a vile attitude or a vile action is for
them the peak of immorality. Impurity, pride, unreliability
seem to them much less grave disvalues than abusing the
trust of another person, or paying back our debts with devalu-
ated money, which may seem correct enough on the surface
but is really a case of plain cheating. They will consider
Father Karamasov to be much worse than Rakitin.

A substitute morality very different from all others, but
perhaps one of the most widespread, is what we may call
"ritualism." We are thinking of all those adherents of a
religion in which certain positive commandments or prohibitions absorb, as it were, the entire realm of morality. To
fulfill these positive commandments means for these people
to fulfill God's will. That *moral* commandments are also
essentially willed by God, that in them we find a call originat-
ing not only in the will of God but also in the very nature
of God, is not understood. The overemphasis on rite and
cult is thus but a step further in the reduction of morality
to positive commandments and prohibitions.

Certain forms of prayers, rites, and cults are regarded as
the only obligatory, serious matter. Compliance with them
becomes the measure which decides the moral worth of a
man. Moreover, we find that with this elimination of morality
in favor of positive commandments and ritual prescriptions,
a tendency to mere exteriorism sets in, that is, a tendency
to deprive all these cultic acts of their very soul. One makes
a substitute morality of a mechanical performance of certain
cultic acts. One believes that such mechanical performance
of prayers, or other ritualistic prescriptions, suffices to placate
the divinity, and thus to insure a good conscience.

Three features characterize this substitute morality. First,
the inner connection between morality and religion is

grasped to some extent. Secondly, morality is restricted to positive commandments. Thirdly, this religious substitute morality is also, from the religious point of view, completely exteriorized and mechanized. The first feature gives this substitute morality a superiority with respect to other substitutes, such as tradition, state law, honor, altruism, insofar as it implies a relation between morality and God. But in connection with the two other features, this advantage is more than counterbalanced by other shortcomings.

The instrumentalization and mechanization which cultic practices have undergone in this substitute morality of ritualism make especially repulsive their claim to spare man all moral requirements. To empty religion of all morality by mechanizing the cultic acts is especially surprising inasmuch as the connection between morality on one hand, and a divinity and religion on the other, is hereby presupposed. It is, however, a typically naïve form of substitute morality. One believes that one can reconcile or satisfy the divinity by these cultic acts. Obviously the offense against God through morally evil things is not understood.

Primarily it is a religious deformation which manifests itself in this substitute morality which we called ritualism. The result of this substitute morality is that morality in its entire material and qualitative content disappears and is replaced by instrumentalized and mechanized cultic practices.

Ritualism, however, occurs not only as a substitute morality, but also as an alleged core of morality. It is in this form that it can become a danger even in the life of certain Catholics in whom the fulfillment of God's commandments shrinks more and more to a strict legality concerning the positive commandments of the Church or to an exteriorized and instrumentalized reception of the sacraments. The question whether one has sinned against charity, justice, or humility does not weigh on these people because the recitation of several rosaries daily gives them the assurance of leading a life which is pleasing to God. We also find at the basis of this type of substitute morality a compromise with pride and concupiscence. By transferring the condition for harmony with God to things which do not challenge pride and concupiscence, or at least not to the same extent as moral commandments, one evades submission to the moral law without suffering a bad conscience.

CHAPTER IV

# NAÏVE AND HERETIC SUBSTITUTES

AFTER THIS BRIEF survey of the main substitutes in the larger and narrower sense, we must still make a general distinction within the sphere of substitutes. Some substitutes bear the seal of naïveté, of an incapacity for distinguishing between moral and extra-moral values. Others bear the seal of distortion and perversion of the moral sphere and moral values which had been known before. One could say that they bear the seal of a kind of "apostasy." We shall term these "heretic" substitutes.

To consider self-control as equivalent to moral goodness can be a result of an incapacity for distinguishing between moral values and those extra-moral personal values which are related in some way to the moral sphere. It can be a blindness due to a view in which the essential differentiation is still lacking, inasmuch as "mores and morality" are not yet fully differentiated. Thus in primitive tribes, tradition and moral norm are confused. In highly cultured peoples also, we find an analogous incapacity when courage, virility, and moral qualities—such as justice and veracity—are regarded as belonging to the same family of values.

The naïve substitutes have the following marks: First, they have no antithetic character. They are not professed and followed with an immanent opposition to other types of morality. For example, the naïve adherents of the substitute of honor, or self-control, or courage, do not manifest this immanent opposition or protest; whereas the ethos of those who identify altruism with morality is filled with indignation against a "false" morality which acknowledges striving for self-perfection and happiness as morally good. Certainly those we have called naïve will react with hostility against those who try to enlighten them in regard to their substitutes and to open their eyes to the true moral law. But this is the general resistance of pride and concupiscence against the realm of true moral values, and the opposition against something "new," "never heard of."

Yet the fact that they oppose "novelties" definitely reveals that their substitute was not pregnant with an opposition and antithesis. The altruist does not oppose what he calls a "selfish" morality because he considers it to be a "novelty"; but, from the very beginning, his substitute implies a protest against this "selfish" morality which, far from being a novelty, is well known to him. The naïve or primitive substitute, on the contrary, does not imply, as such, an immanent protest against other conceptions of morality since there is no conscious selection of this substitute, but rather a confusion of moral and extra-moral values.

Secondly, the naïve substitute is less conscious than the heretic substitutes, as we may call them. In saying "conscious," we do not mean that the conscious apprehension (*prise de conscience*) of the substitute is necessarily lacking in the naïve substitute and only present in the heretic one. For a conscious formulation of the substitute can be found in the naïve substitute as well. But the process itself of building up the substitute is more conscious in the heretic type, since a more conscious decision is implied.

Thirdly, in the naïve substitutes, it is rather an extra-moral value which assumes the role of an exponent and representative of morality; whereas, in the heretic substitutes, it is more a special moral value which is either secularized or isolated, and identified with morality as such.

The difference between naïve and heretic substitutes refers

to an intrinsic difference of mentality which can be found in different stages of civilization.[1]

Thus among highly civilized people, possessing a noble culture—for example, the old Egyptians or even the Greeks of the fifth century B.C.—we find the naïve type of substitutes, that is to say, an absence of a clear distinction between moral and extra-moral values resulting from pride and concupiscence which are at the basis not only of heretic substitutes but of the naïve ones as well. All that thwarts our capacity for distinguishing between moral and extra-moral values is due to pride and concupiscence.[2] All the more, the fact that an extra-moral value becomes the representative of the entire moral sphere betrays the role of pride and concupiscence. The nature of the influence, the specific character of the role of pride and concupiscence, may differ in the cases of the naïve and the heretic substitute; but in both cases the perversion is due to pride and concupiscence.

Fourthly, we have to stress that the naïve and heretic substitutes differ in their qualitative content. Certain substitutes can exist only as naïve, and others only as heretic. The substitutes of self-control and of courage are possible only as naïve substitutes. The substitutes of altruism or of the Tolstoian "warmth of heart" are possible only as heretic ones. We can therefore say that to make of an extra-moral value the substitute for morality is typical of the primitive substitute; whereas to identify one moral value with moral goodness, as such, is typical of the heretic substitute.[3]

[1] In comparing the cultures outside the orbit of the Judeo-Christian revelation with those inside it, we find typical examples of the difference between naïve and heretic substitutes. In the former cultures, we find above all naïve substitutes; in the latter, heretic ones, although not exclusively, as we shall see later on.

[2] This does not apply indiscriminately, as we saw, to the cases of purely traditional value blindness.

[3] If moral apostasy leads to the cult of an extra-moral value, the result is not a substitute for morality but an anti-moral idol. Courage, virility, self-control can also be elements of a Nietzschean "superman." The notion of sage in antiquity sometimes functioned as a substitute for that of the moral

Still more distinctions are necessary in order to clarify the difference between the naïve and the heretic substitutes, especially in order to elaborate the nature of the latter. We sometimes find pagan remnants among Christians, or even relapses to a pagan level, which have, in no way, the character of heretic substitutes. Let us think of the role of honor among the Christian aristocrats in France at the time of Richelieu: so many duels took place among them—fought for the purpose of restoring honor to the offended—that Richelieu introduced the death penalty in an effort to abolish it. Those aristocrats were, nonetheless, Christians, and even felt themselves to be loyal Christians. We do not claim that honor assumed the character of a substitute for morality in the full sense, but it certainly played a vital role, and not as something extra-moral, not merely as a high-ranking objective good for them, similar to life, health, or property, but also as something which they were morally held to defend as a duty.

This is a typical case of a pagan survival in a Christian society, i.e., in those Christians who are not fully converted, inasmuch as they are not fully formed by the Catholic creed.

The ideal of honor survives side by side with the Catholic faith and a loyal attitude toward the commandments of God. These Christians never confront this honor ideal with the commandments of Christ. They neither reach a full awareness of the incompatibility of the two, nor do they try to harmonize them.

In contradistinction to this situation, we find in the errant knight of mediaeval times an attempt to christianize the ideal of honor. The ideal of honor is not a mere remnant which survives, as it were, unchecked and side by side with Christian faith; for there is an attempt to incorporate this remnant into the Christian realm, to elevate and, as it were,

---

personality, but the notion of sage can also assume the character of an anti-moral ideal, against the background of an apostasy from Christianity.

to baptize it. Needless to say, this attempt, though making of honor something much nobler, was futile and foredoomed to failure from the very beginning. This knightly ideal of honor, although nobler, was nevertheless a romantic, poetical conception, and never an authentic Christian one.

From the remnants of paganism, we must distinguish relapses into paganism; and these latter must not be confused with heretic substitutes.

A typical example of relapse into paganism is the notion of the *bien pensant* (the "decent" man). It never has the character of a substitute, which would automatically mean an apostasy from Christ. It is not a substitute for morality, but a norm which, in the life of certain Christians, plays a predominant role, tending to be, practically, even the decisive one. We have called this type of norm not a substitute for morality, but something which is taken as the core of morality. This norm does not have a heretic character, because its adherents have the *will* to be loyal Christians, to obey the commandments of God and of Holy Church. It is rather an unconscious relapse into paganism, an atrophy of their *sensus supranaturalis* or *sensus christianus* which leads to an incapacity for distinguishing natural moral values from extra-moral values and even from mere conventional aspects. Though we are confronted here with a typical process of decay, it has the character of the naïve rather than of the heretic. It is a relapse, but a relapse into primitiveness; and the result has more similarity with the primitive substitute than with the heretical ones.

Even in the case in which honor functions as a substitute and represents morality, as such—for instance, in the case of a Prussian officer—we are not yet confronted with the heretic substitute. Certainly it is a kind of apostasy, because it happens in the Christian realm. But again it has the character of a relapse, though a much more radical relapse than the above-mentioned case. The Christian moral order, even the true natural moral law, is, as it were, forgotten; and something else has been substituted for it. Certain Christian moral values may survive in a distorted form, as remnants, but the existential moral norm is honor. The decisive fact, however, is that the substitute is not a deformation of a Christian or natural moral value, but an extra-moral value, partly even a mere manifestation of pride.

This will become still clearer when turning to the specifically heretic ideals.[4]

To the heretic substitutes belong altruism or the Tolstoian "warmth of heart" and humaneness. The specific features of these substitutes are the following. First, the deformation results primarily from an isolation and overemphasis of a specific value. In picking out one specific moral value and making it the all-embracing general moral value, that is, in identifying morality with it, the moral value in question is necessarily perverted in its very qualitative nature. Secondly, this moral value is opposed, in an aggressive manner, to other moral values as being the only true one. Many moral values

[4] From heretic substitutes, we must, however, distinguish "secularized" ideals. To them belong humanitarian tolerance and the *fraternité* and *égalité* of the French Revolution. (Patently, *fraternité* and *égalité* cannot be equated. The secularization which has taken place in each case is of a very different nature. This difference has been shown admirably by Gabriel Marcel in his work: *Les Hommes contre l'Humain.*) Here we are confronted with Christian notions which have been secularized, that is, deprived of their essential religious basis and, by that, desubstantialized and falsified. These are the typical secularized ideals. (We prescind hereby from the historical question whether behind these deformations there was a budding of a more conscious apprehension of the practical consequences of man's metaphysical dignity.) They are not the result of a relapse, but of a downright apostasy. Their intrinsic deformation does not consist in a falling away from truth, and in substituting for it a remnant of paganism. On the contrary, they are the result of a distortion and radical perversion of a moral value disclosed in the revelation of Christ. What we have here is, as we have said, an apostasy from Christ.

But such secularized ideals are not typical substitutes in our sense, because these *filles égarées* of Christianity are not necessarily substitutes for all morality, that is, representatives of the entire moral sphere. Humanitarians do not always identify moral goodness, as such, with humanitarian fraternity or with tolerance. These ideals do not have, necessarily, the character of a general denominator of morality, though they may also assume this role.

are omitted and overlooked, as in the case of the naïve substitutes; and there are moral values which are even opposed
as being pseudo-morality. This gives to these substitutes an
antithetic, polemic character; they are pregnant with a
"protest." Here we find the typical form of substitutes which
we opposed to the naïve ones, and which we termed heretic.

We see, however, that the heretic substitutes are not
primarily the result of depriving Christian virtues of their
intrinsic religious basis, but of an undue isolation and overemphasis of special Christian virtues. They do not necessarily
imply an apostasy, a formal secularization. We find these
substitutes also among people who still have some religion,
who may even believe themselves to be Christians, perhaps
the only true Christians. But nonetheless a certain apostasy
inevitably takes place here also because the qualitative deformation due to the arbitrary isolation and overemphasis
severs the heretic substitutes from their basis in Christian
revelation, or, as we may say, the qualitative deformation and
perversion *a fortiori* entails a secularization.

However, "heretic" and "naïve" are not strict alternatives.
Some substitutes are not primitive, yet they need not be
heretic in the proper sense of the term, and vice versa. The
man who wants, above all, never to be "base," or who makes
of "genuineness" or "being true to oneself" the core of
morality, does not necessarily derive these notions from
Christian morality. These alleged cores of morality are not
necessarily perversions of Christian virtues. But they have
this in common with the heretic substitutes: they are not
the result of a confusion, but rather of an illegitimate selection. We may term them "decadent" substitutes. The adherents of these substitutes select certain values from the moral
sphere and set up, by that, another norm over the true morally
good and evil.

This procedure shares with the heretic the character of
decadence, a retrograde movement and an antithetic tendency. This latter feature is not so outspoken in decadent

substitutes as in heretic ones. But the decadent substitutes also imply, at least, a certain invalidating of all other moral values. In saying only "genuineness" really counts, or in claiming that the only important thing is, morally speaking, to avoid anything "vile," one chooses a special moral value (as in the heretic), and not an extra-moral one, as a substitute for morality. This choice is not rooted in a primitive ignoring of many moral values, for it presupposes the knowledge of the moral sphere. But in making of a special moral value a substitute for morality, a gesture of brushing the other moral values aside is inevitably implied.

The distinction between naïve, heretic, and decadent substitutes patently has a bearing on the genesis of the substitute. The role of extra-moral values in the naïve substitutes, and of special isolated moral values in decadent and heretic substitutes, clearly points to this fact. We shall deal with these three groups separately, and each one of them will make different analyses necessary.

## CHAPTER V

## EXTRA-MORAL VALUES

WE SAW THAT substitutes are the result of a compromise. On the one hand, a link with the moral sphere subsists in them; on the other, a concession is made to pride and concupiscence. We saw further that in the case of primitive substitutes certain extra-moral values assume the role of morally good and evil.

The role of extra-moral values in the realm of primitive substitutes, and the *reason* why they assume this role, will now be our topic. Yet before beginning this analysis, we must enlarge upon a distinction in the realm of values made in *Christian Ethics*. In that work, we distinguished between qualitative and ontological values. The human person possesses, first, an ontological value as image of God, a value which every man possesses equally. But the human person may possess many qualitative values or disvalues, such as vital, intellectual, and especially moral values and disvalues, for example, charm, wit, purity, justice, clumsiness, impurity, etc.; and it is with respect to these qualitative values or disvalues that there exist great differences between individual persons. Yet we have still to make a further distinction.

As we saw in *Christian Ethics*,[1] not only substances possess an ontological value. Thus, not only man, as such, but also his intelligence and his free will, that is to say, his different capacities, have a high ontological value. They are in themselves something precious and noble. Free will is, as such,

---

[1] Cf. *Christian Ethics*, p. 133.

a great, sublime entity; though only the will which is a response to morally relevant goods is endowed with a qualitative—in this case, a moral—value.

Yet when we praise the strength of will of a person, his energy, and his capacity to control his instincts and impulses by means of his will, we are concerned neither with the ontological value of will as such nor with the qualitative values which are to be found in every man, but with a specific perfection of this capacity which is not to be found in every man. The same is the case when we praise someone for his acuteness and sharpness of intellect. For we are then concerned with a specific perfection of the intellect, which is not to be found in every man and which is present in many different degrees in those who possess it. These values, based on a specific perfection of a capacity, are not identical with the ontological value of the capacity, as such; but they also differ from the qualitative values, such as moral goodness, humility, justice; or, intellectual depth, being rooted in truth, knowing truth. The values based on a perfection of a capacity, such as energy, self-control, strength of will, differ from the qualitative value by their immanence. They are based on the merely immanent perfection of a capacity, its full functioning, and not on the participation in something transcendent.

In comparing the strength of will with the moral goodness of will the fundamental difference between the two types of values clearly discloses itself. The moral goodness of will is, in no way, an immanent perfection of an act of willing. It can never be understood or grasped if we remain in the frame of the immanent perfection of the will, its *technically* efficient functioning, as it were. We have, on the contrary, to question to which good the act of willing is directed, which kind of importance motivates the act of willing, and, in the case of a value response, which kind of value motivates this value response. We have to look at something beyond the immanent logic of the act of willing, at something which utterly transcends it, in order to be able to distinguish between a morally good and a morally evil volitional response.

The qualitative values differ, thus, from those values of perfection by their transcendence. But apart from this fundamental difference, they also have a completely different qualitative plenitude. Compared with the moral goodness of will, mere strength of will or an energetic will is something rather formal and technical. It has the character of an instrumental perfection. Something analogous is to be found in the intellectual sphere. The sharpness and acuteness of thinking, the perfection which we may also acknowledge in a philosopher whose thought is basically vitiated by errors, e.g., a skeptic, a positivist, a logicist, a relativist, clearly differ from the intellectual depth and luminous penetration of a philosopher who discovers basic truths. In comparing the intelligence of a St. Augustine with the intelligence of a Bertrand Russell, we find, in both, formal acuteness and sharpness of intellect; but only in St. Augustine do we find depth, beauty, and luminosity of intellect—values which the mind can acquire only when it is sustained by the light of truth, which of course cannot be separated from truth on the side of the object, and its function of forming the intellect.

If we have to distinguish the values based on an immanent perfection from the qualitative values, we must, as mentioned above, equally distinguish them from the ontological values. The ontological values, in the proper sense of the term, are characterized by this that they are embodied in the very essence of a being, and that every individual being possessing this essence possesses this value, and to the same degree. Every man is an image of God and is endowed with the same ontological dignity, which is proper to each personal creature. Every act of willing embodies the ontological value which the will, as such, a weak one as well as a strong one, possesses. The value of a strong or energetic will, on the contrary, is obviously something which is found in some persons and not in others.

It seems, then, that there exist three fundamentally different types of values: the ontological values, the technical values, the qualitative values. First, the ontological values of the different beings, whether they are substances or not. Secondly, the values which are based on the immanent perfections of certain beings.[2] Thirdly, the qualitative values which form different families, under the heading of moral, aesthetic, and intellectual. The second type of values, which differs from the ontological as well as from the qualitative values in a decisive way, shares certain essential features with the ontological, others with the qualitative ones.

These values of the second type share with the ontological values the character of immanence. Moreover, in order to grasp them, we must know the ontological value of the being in question, human, subhuman, etc. The value of an energetic, strong will, of a will able to dominate the impulses and instincts, can be grasped only if we have already understood the nature of will and its ontological value. The perfection is the fulfillment of an immanent intention of this being, and is intimately linked to the ontological value. It is thus clearly opposed to the transcendence of the qualitative values.

Like the ontological values, the technical values are not classified in different families. Such a classification is a specific characteristic of the qualitative values only. Like ontological values, the technical values are centered around a specific type of being; and their specific nature is to such an extent linked to the type of being and its ontological value that its difference from other values of this sort is primarily determined by the nature of this being. Strength of will, energy, self-control are, in their *forma,* determined by the immanent nature of will.

But they share with the qualitative values the following

---

[2] These values of immanent perfection are especially stressed by Aristotle, whereas Plato is primarily concerned with qualitative values.

marks: First, they are not, like ontological values, proper to every being of a certain species, but they are present in one individual, absent in another; and when they are present, they are embodied in one individual more than in another. Thus we can speak of a weak will, or a strong one, of a stronger and less strong will; we can distinguish between an acute intellect and one which is weak, confused, or between one which is acute and one which is less so.

We saw in *Christian Ethics* that one of the characteristic differences between ontological and qualitative values consists in the fact that there are no disvalues forming an antithesis to ontological values, whereas to every qualitative value there corresponds a disvalue which constitutes its contrary antithesis.

There is no disvalue which would correspond antithetically to the ontological value of a human person. Here we can speak only of the presence or absence of this value. A plant does not have the ontological value of a person, but it does not thereby embody a disvalue; on the contrary, it also has an ontological value, though a much lower one. To the qualitative value of moral goodness, on the contrary, corresponds antithetically the disvalue of moral badness; and to beauty corresponds ugliness.

If we analyze the values of perfection (technical values) from this angle, we see that they, too, have a contrary antithesis. We oppose heavy-mindedness to acuteness of intellect; we oppose weakness of will, irresolution, or inhibitedness to energy and strength of will. They are obviously disvalues and form an antithesis to the positive values. Yet the nature of the antithesis still differs from the one which we find in the realm of qualitative values for it has the character of a privation. Thus, weakness of will can also be considered a very low degree of strength of will; whereas patently malicious wickedness cannot be looked at as a low degree of charity. These hints may suffice to introduce this third fundamental type of values which we termed technical or instrumental values.[3]

Our inquiry, at present, refers to such extra-moral values which are sometimes confused with moral values or which have such a relation to the moral sphere that they are likely to be confused with moral values. Values which can never be embodied in a person, such as many aesthetic values (e.g., the dramatic, the beauty of a quartet or of a novel), are out of question here. Among the values whose bearer can be a person, we have again to eliminate such technical and qualitative values which in their theme and quality lack any affinity with the moral sphere. Technical values such as good memory and acuteness of intellect are obviously too remote from the moral sphere ever to be confused with moral values. Again, qualitative values such as wittiness, sense of humor, temperamental "charm" are so remote from the moral sphere that a confusion with moral values is also out of question. Whereas a technical value such as strength of will, or a qualitative value such as courage, may be confused with moral values.

In analyzing those extra-moral values which are likely to be confused with moral values, we have really a twofold aim. One is to elaborate the role of extra-moral values in the formation of substitutes for morality. The other is the further elaboration of moral and morally relevant values [4] in contradistinction to all other values, or the further elaboration of the moral sphere and of the moral theme.

The precise and clear-cut distinction between moral and extra-moral values is not only indispensable for the understanding of the nature and genesis of the substitutes, but is also, as such, a fundamental task for ethics.

[3] In a later work, the nature of this type of values will be minutely analyzed.

[4] In *Christian Ethics*, Chapter 17, we elaborated the nature of moral values in contradistinction to all other types of values; and we referred to the difference between morally relevant and morally irrelevant values in Chapter 18 of the same work.

We discussed the character of moral values in general in *Christian Ethics*. Now we have to elaborate further the nature of moral values *in concreto* by showing their difference from other values; we must especially unmask as extra-moral values such values as are often considered to be moral ones. To sharpen the sense for the specific nature of moral values, to increase the *sapere* of their flavor and quality, is a paramount end of true ethics.[5]

Extra-moral personal values which are often confused with moral values are, above all: self-control, energy, and courage. They will be our topic in the following analysis.

Aristotle considers self-control to be one of the main moral values.[6] Without any doubt it is an indispensable element in any virtuous man. To be unable to dominate our passions and inclinations with our will is certainly incompatible with being virtuous. But, on the other hand, our being able to control our passions, inclinations, and instincts with the will in no way guarantees moral goodness. An enemy of God may also possess great self-control. Among morally evil persons some are prey to their passions, letting themselves be ruled by them without any resistance or control by reason and will. But such persons were considered as brutelike and fools by Aristippus of Cyrene, the ancient hedonist who himself taught a doctrine of self-control. He opposed to them the wise man who, while pursuing the agreeable, does not let himself be dominated by his passions and desires, but controls them with his reason and his will. He also claimed that self-control is indispensable to wisdom. But the same Aristippus of Cyrene nevertheless declared that only a fool will let himself be impeded in the pursuit of pleasure by considerations which,

---

[5] This second scope explains our insistence on the distinction between moral and extra-moral courage in the latter part of this chapter which may seem out of proportion from the point of view of the substitutes for morality. Extra-moral courage plays no specific role in the building up of substitutes, certainly not more than many others. But it is very often listed as moral value and thus yields itself especially to this second task.

[6] Aristotle, *Nicomachean Ethics*.

expressed in our terminology, would refer to moral commandments and moral values. Adultery, sacrilegious thefts, murder are all completely legitimate if the pleasure which they convey is greater than the displeasure which we may incur on their account.

Clearly, then, self-control, as such, in no way guarantees the basic morally good direction of the will. For, as we can see, we find among morally evil persons, not only the man who is prey to his passions and instincts, but also the man who pursues the satisfaction of his pride, ambition, and concupiscence in a reasonable way (using the term "reasonable" in the sense of Aristippus) and possesses a high degree of self-control. A Richard III (in the Shakespearean conception) possessed this self-control, whereas Father Karamasov is a typical case of one who is subject to his passions, lacking every self-control.

We must not be deceived by the argument that Richard III and Rakitin did not possess self-control because they were dominated by their pride and, instead of aiming at their true happiness, they allowed themselves to be controlled by their pride.

This argument is based on an equivocation. The terms "self-control" and "reason" are used in two different senses. In the first, it refers to the capacity of our will to control and dominate our impulsive tendencies, for instance, to abstain in a given situation from the satisfaction of a desire, be it lechery or greediness or the desire to take revenge or a fit of anger.[7] In the other sense, self-control is contrasted with enslavement to pride and concupiscence, insofar as our will,

---

[7] Plato had a similar thought in mind when he wrote: "Then all but the philosophers are courageous only from fear, and because they are afraid.... And are not the temperate exactly in the same case? They are temperate because they are intemperate.... For there are pleasures which they are afraid of losing, and in their desire to keep them, they abstain from some pleasures because they are overcome by others...." *Phaedo*, translated by Jowett (New York: Random House), p. 452.

in refusing to submit to them, is directed to the realm of morally relevant values or ultimately to God.

Patently, these are two radically different meanings of self-control. In the latter meaning, it is not a mere question of "strength" or the merely formal capacity to submit everything to our will; in short, it is not simply a matter of technical perfection. This latter meaning refers rather to the right use of our freedom concerning motivation or the category of importance by which we let ourselves be motivated. It has to do with the question whether our will is a value response or merely a response to the subjectively satisfying. It refers to the great, basic moral decision whether our will is directed to God or to our "flesh" (here equivalent to pride and concupiscence)—a decision which St. Augustine stressed time and again.

To us, it seems very unfortunate to apply the term "self-control" to this victory of our value-responding center over pride and concupiscence, to this most qualitative decision. For it is completely illegitimate to identify a moral victory with the merely formal and technical domination by our will. At any rate, the two things in question have to be clearly distinguished, whatever terminology one chooses.

The same applies to the use of "reasonable" in both these cases. On one hand, we call reasonable the man who conforms to the immanent logic of the end he has chosen, contrasting him with one who simply follows his instincts and passionate desires. The term "reasonable" in this sense is applicable to the man who conforms to the famous prescription of Aristippus, who chooses the more intense pleasure, the longer lasting, the one which entails no displeasure afterward and which can be attained with less strain and with greater probability. This "reasonable" man is here contrasted with the fool who, without making use of his reason, runs in a brutelike manner after his pleasure. Another time, one calls "reasonable" the man who understands the primacy of a value with respect to all the merely subjectively satisfying;

who stands in the truth; who knows that, above all, he should respond to the morally relevant values and that true happiness is a gift which can be attained only if we "seek first the kingdom of God and His justice."

Thus we see that self-control in the strict sense, though indispensable for the attainment of virtue, is not, as such, a guarantee of morality, since in itself it does not embody a specific moral value. It is a value, undoubtedly; and has even a great bearing on moral goodness, as an instrument. But it may also bring about an increase of moral wickedness.[8] A criminal with self-control or an enemy of God is even more wicked and terrible than a man who follows his passions in a brutelike way; he is certainly more satanic; he has greater similarity to Lucifer.

Someone could object: The fact that a virtue is to be found in a man whose basic direction of will is morally evil is no proof of its extra-moral character. Do we not sometimes find in criminals elements of compassion or faithfulness and loyalty to a comrade? There can be no doubt about the moral character of compassion or faithfulness. Hence the fact that self-control can be found also in the evil man, in the enemy of God, is no proof that self-control is no moral value.

To this objection, we must answer: It is not the mere fact that a value can be found in a morally evil person which proves its extra-moral character, but rather the way in which it "coexists" with the basic evil direction of will. In the case of a criminal who feels compassion or who would rather suffer than betray his comrade, these attitudes clearly contradict his general moral habit. They surprise us and raise a problem which we try to explain.[9] But when we find

---

[8] Plato writes: "... your zeal is invaluable, if a right one; but if wrong, the greater the zeal, the greater the danger..." *Crito*, translated by Jowett (New York: Random House, Vol. I), p. 430.

[9] In these cases, it is either a temporary breakthrough, so that the exclusive domination of pride and concupiscence is suspended for a moment, or

courage or self-control in an enemy of God, there is, on the contrary, no contradiction between these qualities and his moral evilness. Neither do they surprise us, nor do they confront us with a mystery. Moreover, there is no contradiction; far from it, for self-control, energy, and courage even enhance, as we saw before, the moral evilness of actions. The enemy of God who has self-control, courage, and energy is even more wicked than the one who lacks these qualities; as we have said, he is more Lucifer-like.

This could never be said of the compassion felt by a criminal, or of his faithfulness to and solidarity with his comrades. These qualities, far from increasing his moral wickedness, have definitely the character of bright spots, of things which could be mentioned in his favor from a moral point of view. Thus we can see that the coexistence of basic moral evilness and personal values, without inner contradiction or conflict, definitely proves that these personal values are not of a moral character. Above all, the fact that these personal values not only coexist amiably, but even increase moral evilness, is a clear indication of their extra-moral character.

We see then that self-control is not a moral value but a formal technical one. It increases the moral goodness in a man whose basic direction of will is good. Likewise, it also increases the moral wickedness in a man whose basic direction of will is evil. Yet, surprisingly enough, the absence of self-control is not only the absence of a formal technical value, but is also a *moral* disvalue. In order to understand this fact we must, however, probe still further regarding the nature of self-control.

In speaking of self-control, we must distinguish three main different forms. The first is the technical dominion of the will over our passions, impulses, and instincts. The ability

---

the morally good qualities are remnants whose presence can be attributed to the rather unconscious character of the criminal's nature. On the other hand, these qualities have never the character of full moral virtues.

to command every action, and even every expression of our instincts, passions, and emotions, and our affective responses, though potentially proper to every man, is in some persons highly developed. They have by education, practice, and routine attained such a dominion over themselves that their will is able to sap the expression of their anger, their enthusiasm, their fear, their joy, their sorrow, their violent desire, their envy, their impatience. They always have themselves in hand; they not only can abstain from following their impulses insofar as the sphere of action is concerned, but they can also suppress all those impulsive expressions of what they feel and think; they can even dissemble their inner life to such an extent that their expression and demeanor may be just the opposite of what goes on in their soul and mind.

Self-control in this sense has a technical character; it belongs to the technical values, insofar as it is a mere perfection of the will concerning the functioning of its commanding capacity. But it is definitely not yet a moral value. In saying a person has a high degree of self-control, we do not yet indicate whether he is a virtuous man or an enemy of God or a criminal. Likewise, when someone is presented to us as possessing a high degree of self-control, we do not yet know what he is from the moral point of view.

We also find this kind of self-control in persons who are neither enemies of God nor especially virtuous men, but very efficient personalities, whose self-control is helpful to them in their professional life and in attaining different ends.

Self-control in this sense is definitely *not* a moral value. What a difference there is between such self-control and the domination of pride and concupiscence in the depth of our being by freeing ourselves from their fangs! The latter is never a mere matter of the formal functioning of the commanding power of our will for it has to do with a qualitative ultimate decision which uses our freedom in the right way. It is possible only as the fruit of our free value response to the good and, ultimately, to God. It is the free actualization of the reverent, humble, loving center in us, very remote from the mere technical perfection of our will in its commanding role.

When technical self-control is used by a will responding to morally relevant goods, it assumes, besides its formal technical value, an indirect moral value. A man who has self-control may avoid giving offense to others when angry, whereas a man having the same good intention, but lacking self-control, may not be able to do so. Self-control is of course indispensable for virtue. If someone possesses self-control as a temperamental disposition, or has acquired it (yet not for *moral* motives), he may place it at the disposal of a morally good will, whenever the moral theme calls for it.

But in the morally conscious person possessing a basic general will to be good, self-control assumes a completely new character. It is no longer the mere technical perfection of being in command, but is now part of the striving for moral goodness. It is inspired by the desire to conform to the moral law and the moral commandments and to dwell on the path of the Lord. The virtuous man wants to control his impulses and his passions, not for the sake of self-control or self-dominion, but in order to avoid going morally astray. Such control assumes, above all, the character of a fight against concupiscence, for, if he permitted himself to be ruled by his tendencies, impulses, or instincts, he would be making a concession to it.

In the morally conscious virtuous man, self-control assumes the character of *habitare secum* (dwelling in one's depth). One refuses to indulge in spiritual laziness and to yield to the satisfaction of concupiscence, both of which underlie a lack of self-control. We can clearly see the decisive difference between this moral self-control of the virtuous man and the above-mentioned technical self-control, independently of whether this technical self-control is used as an instrument for greater efficiency (as, for example, in professional life) or is used as a means for something morally good.

Technical or instrumental self-control is, in itself, a personal value, but not a moral one. It assumes an indirect moral value when used as a means for something morally relevant. But self-control in the morally conscious virtuous man has itself a moral value, because of its qualitatively different character. In neutral self-control we aim at mastery over ourselves; in moral self-control we intend to become better servants of God.

We can now understand why the absence of self-control is always a moral disvalue—because from a moral point of view we should not let our natural tendencies develop and express themselves unchecked and uncontrolled. Every lack of self-control has even a direct morally negative connotation, insofar as it embodies a letting ourselves go. But as we saw, the presence of self-control does not always have even an indirect moral value. So long as it is only technical self-control it has no moral value; when it is a means used by a morally good will, it assumes an indirect moral value. Only the self-control of the virtuous man inspired and formed by the basic moral value response is directly endowed with a moral value.

The absence of self-control implies a direct moral disvalue. The morally good man who is striving to dwell on the paths of the Lord, and who still has a low degree of self-control (it may be that he is unable to control a great fit of anger or of impatience, or that he cannot yet control his nerves; it may be that he simply lets himself go and laughs too much or speaks too much: both of which are, in themselves, morally innocent), will himself consider it a moral guilt, registering it in his conscience as such.

Mastery over self, in order to be more efficient in obtaining satisfaction of pride and concupiscence, is again another form of self-control.[10] This self-control assumes even a morally

[10] Something analogous is to be found in the extra-moral value of energy. To be energetic is certainly better than not to be so. Apart from having a value, as such, energy also is a factor in the increase of moral perfection.

evil character; it increases wickedness and makes a man more Lucifer-like.

Strictly speaking, self-control can be found in five different forms:

First, self-control as the mere skill or dexterity of the will; the immanent efficient functioning of the will in its capacity to command. As such it is a technical, personal value, but it is definitely not a moral value. It is neutral from the moral point of view.

Secondly, technical self-control which is used as an instrument by a morally good will. It is no longer morally neutral, because, placed at the disposal of a morally relevant good, it assumes an indirect moral value.

Thirdly, the self-control which is a consequence of our preoccupation to avoid going morally astray; and which is, moreover, an element of the *habitare secum* and a victory over concupiscence, insofar as one refuses to let himself go, to indulge his inclinations. This is the completely different moral self-control, which has no longer a technical character, which draws its strength from morally relevant values at stake, and ultimately from the love of God.

---

The good man who is energetic will achieve more, and will attain a higher perfection, than the one who is lacking energy. But energy, in itself, is no moral value; and we find energetic people also among evildoers, criminals, and enemies of God.

Like self-control, energy in itself is a technical value, and in no way a moral value, such as, for instance, veracity, justice, or purity. However, to be energetic is an advantage from the moral point of view, an augmenting factor, if the man is basically good, if he has the general will to be good. But it also makes the evil man still worse.

And again we must distinguish between mere formal energy and the strength of will inspired by the morally relevant value to which the will is directed. The second is endowed with a moral value, whereas the first has merely an extra-moral value, or, in the best of cases, an indirect moral value.

However, the relation between energy and the moral sphere is only analogous to that between self-control and the moral sphere. Energy is still more instrumental than self-control, and it appears often as a temperamental disposition. But because of its relation to the moral sphere it is sometimes believed to be a moral value.

Fourthly, technical self-control which is occasionally used as an instrument for attaining a morally illegitimate end. It then assumes an indirect moral disvalue. It increases the efficacy of evil.

Finally, the self-control of the morally evil man which increases his wickedness because of its character as a more conscious and outspoken rebellion against the moral law. It is here a definite, moral disvalue; it is poisoned by the moral wickedness of the man's basic direction of will and makes him, consequently, still more Lucifer-like than the evil man without self-control.

We see thus the different relations of self-control to the moral sphere (though in itself self-control is an extra-moral technical value of the person). Later on we shall see the specific attractiveness of this extra-moral value for pride. We shall then understand why—for example, in the Stoic morality—self-control becomes a kind of substitute for the moral sphere.

Another extra-moral personal value which is not a technical but rather a qualitative one is courage. We are thinking of the quality which is praised in many heroes, the fact that someone does not fear danger, that he dares cope with danger and risks of all kinds.

In speaking of courage many different attitudes must be distinguished, which are covered by this term. The first and most decisive difference is that between extra-moral courage and the moral courage which is rooted in a moral value response. Extra-moral courage is to be found, for instance, in an Alexander the Great; moral courage in David, when he fights Goliath.

Later on, we shall deal with the nature of moral courage. For the moment we prescind from it, because in our present inquiry we are concerned with extra-moral personal values and their relation to the moral sphere.

In the frame of extra-moral courage, we must, from the very beginning, distinguish courage with respect to exterior dangers and risks (i.e., "physical courage," as we term it sometimes in a rather incorrect way) from courage with respect to spiritual dangers. We praise the former in a man who is courageous in a battle, in a fire, in a storm, or who scales mountain peaks, or goes hunting for big game. The second we praise in a man who speaks up, even when the uttering of his opinion may bring great disadvantages to him, or who courageously endures the loss of his property and his being reduced to poverty. Again we praise it in a man who is free from "human respect" and does not depend in his attitudes upon other people's opinions.

Let us consider, first, extra-moral physical courage. Here again we have to distinguish two main types: temperamental physical courage, which is a natural disposition to cope with exterior dangers, and physical courage which is the result of a strong will.

A prototype of temperamental physical courage is Siegfried in Wagner's opera, *Die Nibelungen.* Fear is unknown to him. He cannot even imagine the nature of this feeling. He leaves the grotto of Mime in order to learn "fear." Many different elements may determine this temperamental courage, either one of them or many together. The first is the childlike blindness to dangers, the fact that one is not even aware of them. This is usually associated with a lack of imagination. One is not able to form vivid images of all the possible dangers. This "courage" is a result of a strong vitality, but it must not be linked with a strong vitality in any necessary way.

The second is the feeling that one can cope with potential dangers even when they are seen. This temperamental courage is always rooted in a superabundant vitality which engenders the feeling that one can and will overcome the difficulties, and may even make one optimistic enough to believe that the potential dangers will not occur. This superabundant vitality may sometimes be of such a character that one even enjoys being confronted with dangers, finding a special source of satisfaction in the consciousness of mastering difficult and dangerous exterior situations. This is the case with the type who indulges in dangerous sports or who approaches fortuitous dangers in a sporting manner.

This temperamental courage is a value; it is certainly as such preferable to timorousness in the face of every exterior danger. But, patently, it is not a moral value. Morally speaking, there is no difference between the temperamental courageous type and the timorous type.

Temperamental courage is a value belonging to the group of vital values, such as vivacity, strong temperament, and plenitude of life. It has also a specific aesthetic charm.

From this temperamental physical courage we must distinguish the physical courage which is the result of a strong will. Someone may have poor vitality and, in clearly grasping dangers surrounding him in a special situation, may be intimidated by them. But he controls his fear with his will and, in spite of his fear, he achieves what he has decided to do.

An acrobat whose performances are perilous may be timorous by disposition, but his desire for fame is so strong that in overcoming his fear with his will, he does violence to his nature.

The coping with an exterior dangerous situation, whether by a sailor or an auto-racer or an acrobat or a mountain "climber" or a "stunt-flyer," may be supported by temperamental courage, but it may also be exclusively the result of a strong will which faces dangers in spite of a temperamental timorousness. It, too, will be called courage, though the value in question has a completely different character from temperamental courage. In contrast to the superabundant vitality which constitutes Siegfried's charm, it is much more akin to self-control and energy. Yet it has a new quality, with respect to them, because of the specific relation to dangers. It has definitely a value which is not yet a moral value, although it has a more spiritual value than mere temperamental courage. Because of the "feat" of the will in-cluded in this type of courage, it is often confused with moral courage, and even considered as having a moral value.

But, in fact, this kind of courage need have no relation to morally relevant goods. For men may risk life or limb only in order to be famous. There even exist men who are motivated by pride alone in overcoming their timorousness, because they cannot bear to see themselves in so miserable a light. Even in the criminal, in the basically amoral man, or in the enemy of God, we find this kind of courage, and not only the kind we call temperamental.

After having dealt with temperamental physical courage, and the physical courage which results from strength of will, both of them extra-moral values, we turn to that type of extra-moral courage which, in contradistinction to physical courage, refers to man's relation to dangers pertaining to the psychic sphere or any kind of intimidating elements in the social order.

This courage differs to such an extent from physical cour-age that the presence of physical courage in no way guaran-tees its presence. We may say that physical courage and this inner courage are completely independent of each other. Not only does the one not guarantee the other, but the former does not even facilitate the latter. Many persons with great physical courage fear poverty or the loss of their money, nor will they dare to oppose public opinion or the opinion of a strong personality; they will remain silent when they should speak up, or they are prey to "human respect."

Again in the frame of this inner courage, we must dis-tinguish the temperamental form from the one based on a strong will. Because of their strong vitality, certain persons have a feeling of security with respect to the vicissitudes of life. They do not worry about the future; they are not con-cerned with the outcome of impending trials or difficulties; they live to such an extent in their present work or pleasures that they give not a thought to tomorrow and its ordeals.

But even when these ordeals descend on them, even when they lose their money and are deprived of the normal basis of their existence, they remain courageous, without giving way to depression and without losing their head. The opposite of this temperamental courage is found in the man who worries continuously about the future, who fears poverty and insecurity and is crushed by them. Temperamental inner courage has an aesthetic charm; besides, it is, as such, a vital value. But obviously it is not a moral value.[11]

Another brand of inner courage in the frame of temperamental dispositions is to be found in the person who, because of his strong personality, his independent original mind, is not impressed by public opinion nor by the opinions of other strong personalities. He may even not "care a fig" for the opinion of others. He will thus speak up and utter his opinion regardless of the uproar that may result. His strength or independence is undoubtedly something positive. It has a value though not yet a moral one. We may call him courageous because he does not fear to be despised, laughed at,

[11] Notwithstanding its vital value this type of courage may, however, have a negative connotation. It may lead to thoughtlessness, and is often combined with carelessness. From this vital value of temperamental courage, we must therefore distinguish also another extra-moral value, a reasonable attitude toward the vicissitudes and dangers of life. It is unreasonable either to be thoughtless regarding possible vicissitudes, or to be too much concerned with possible difficulties. To have a temperamental disposition which keeps the *via media* between carelessness and apprehensiveness is the real extra-moral value here in question. It is to this domain of extra-moral values that the Aristotelian *mesotes* theory really applies. We say extra-moral, because the man who has this reasonable attitude toward the vicissitudes of life as the result of a healthy, normal temperament does not thereby embody a moral value. He may be a vicious man, his basic direction of will may be an immoral one, and yet he may have—due to his temperament—a reasonable attitude toward the vicissitudes of life. Thus we see how the *via media* here leads us to a reasonable attitude, which is the one a man should have. But this "should" has to do with reasonability in general and is not the oughtness of morality.

Cf. *Christian Ethics*, Chapter 16. Yet we shall see in the last chapter of this book how attitudes which on the natural level are endowed only with an extra-moral value may assume an indirect moral value in the frame of Christian morality.

or contradicted. He does not even boggle at disadvantages of all kinds which may be the consequence of his attitude. Something similar is the absence of "human respect." The independence or strength which this courage includes is definitely something positive, it has a value. But we may find it also in morally evil persons, and it increases their immorality, making them more satanic. It has, thus, only as such, an extra-moral value.

The different types of inner courage can also be found as qualities of the will, instead of being temperamental dispositions. There are people who are aware of potential vicissitudes, and are not thoughtless and careless in their temperamental disposition, and who still control their apprehensiveness with their strong will. We praise them as brave and courageous. But here also it is not necessarily a moral value at which we hint with these terms. It may be a wicked man who has this strength of will, who copes with all kinds of trials in the pursuit of his ambitious goals. The same applies to the man who has overcome his natural timidity and, because of his strong will, speaks up and says what he thinks.

We also find persons who, because of certain aims which they want passionately to attain, will overcome with their will the human respect which is strong in them. In order to satisfy their ambition or to win the admiration of a person whom they love, they will, in spite of their "human respect," do things which make them "ridiculous."

Moral courage clearly differs from all these types of courage, physical or inner courage, temperamental courage or that which is the result of a strong will. The characteristic of this courage is that it is born out of a response to a morally relevant good. Coping with a physical danger assumes a completely new character when a morally relevant good is at stake which can be saved only by facing up to the danger, and when the attitude toward the danger is formed and inspired by the response to the morally relevant good. The man who risks his life in order to save his neighbor is courageous in a completely new sense if in coping with danger he is inspired by the impact of the moral theme in question. Then courage is an outgrowth of the moral value response.

Yet we must also distinguish between two different forms of courage from the moral point of view: the morally neutral courage which facilitates a morally good action involving the surmounting of dangers, and moral courage proper. Morally neutral courage assumes an indirect moral value when it serves as a means of accomplishing something morally good. It assumes an indirect moral disvalue when it is used for accomplishing morally evil things. In itself, it is merely an extra-moral value.

Moral courage, on the other hand, is engendered by the moral call in question and is fruit of the love of God. It is itself endowed with a moral value.

The courage which is a moral virtue can be found in men who lack extra-moral courage as well as in those who have it. It may be easier for the man having a temperamental physical courage, but we find many examples in history of morally courageous deeds achieved by temperamentally timorous men.

In any case, moral courage is present when an exterior danger is faced for the sake of a morally relevant good. Moral courage is the ardor of the value response which overcomes fear, and is therefore impossible so long as no morally relevant good is in question.

The same applies to moral inner courage. To risk all kinds of vicissitudes, such as poverty, persecution, because of the call of a morally relevant good, or because the alternative is either to sin or to accept these objective evils for us, is moral courage; and such courage obviously differs in its quality and character from temperamental inner courage or the inner courage which is a result of a mere technical strength of will. Again, if someone speaks up, because the situation morally calls for it, courage to disregard public opinion and the violent uproar which it may cause has a completely new character, for it is inspired and supported by the moral call, and is a fruit of a response to a morally relevant good.

To disregard all human respect in doing what we are morally obliged to do or what is morally good is an act of moral courage. The disregard of "human respect" assumes, patently, a completely new character when it arises from a value response instead of from a merely temperamental independence and from indifference toward one's own social image, or when it results from a technical strength of will, as in the case of a man who disregards all human respect for the sake of something subjectively satisfying.

But it is not this completely different moral courage which is our specific topic, but rather extra-moral courage and its relation to pride and concupiscence.

Our analysis has shown, first of all, that self-control and courage, as such, are not moral values. This distinction helped us indirectly to elaborate further the specific nature of moral values, to throw into greater relief their qualitative quiddity. This is the above-mentioned second purpose of our present analysis. Needless to say, it surpasses in its import our immediate topic which is the nature and genesis of substitutes.

Secondly, we also understand now why those personal values are often confused with moral values. Yet often these extra-moral values are not only erroneously considered to be moral values; they even function sometimes as substitutes for morality. The same applies with respect to several other extra-moral values, especially all those which underlie the alternative "honorable or dishonorable," and which are the typical requirements of honor.[12] However, in order to understand why certain extra-moral values assume the role of

---

[12] In the lived morality of the Stoic (not to the same extent in his ethics, i.e., his philosophical theories on morality) self-control in the form of ἀπάθεια ο ἀταραχια (apathy or ataraxy) assumes the character of a general denominator for morality.

substitutes, further inquiries are necessary. We must study their relation to pride and concupiscence, and show why they are more acceptable to pride and concupiscence than the true moral values and the true moral norm. We must analyze why these extra-moral values lend themselves to compromise: maintaining a link to the sphere of morality while escaping the full challenge to pride and concupiscence.

## CHAPTER VI

## EXTRA-MORAL VALUES AND PRIDE

WE SAW IN CHAPTER II that a fundamental demarcation must be made between the attitude of the proud man toward values in general and his attitude toward moral values. It is now imperative to throw this fundamental demarcation into greater relief. The value blindness rooted in pride refers to all values, but above all to moral values. However, another degree of pride is presupposed in blindness to the value of intelligence, or energy or self-control, than that which is presupposed in blindness to moral values.

Satanic pride blinds one to all values.[1] And the very existence of a value is experienced as a spoliation of one's own glory. The higher the rank of the value, the more will this feeling of spoliation grow, but this will take place in a specific way with respect to moral values.

Natural moral values are already a scandal to satanic pride; they constitute an antithesis to pride in a completely new manner, not to be compared with the one all other types of values embody. Their mysterious "glory" is a declaration of war on pride; they contradict pride in a unique way. Yet a completely new stage of incompatibility is reached in Christian morality. For pride has to abdicate completely before Christ, and the proud man has to go down on his knees.

We prescind at present from satanic pride [2] and turn to less radical, less deeply rooted forms of pride.

As we have already seen in Chapter II, in these less virulent forms, some proper estimate of the importance of extra-moral

[1] We shall see later on in what sense this blindness is to be understood.
[2] Cf. *Christian Ethics.*

84

values can be found. The ambitious type who craves power and influence over other persons may have a certain understanding of intellectual values, aesthetic values, or extra-moral personal values. He may admire a man because of his intelligence or a work of art because of its beauty. He may, above all, admire someone for his energy and self-control.

Granted that his approach to these values will always be tainted insofar as he would like to make them his own for the sake of self-glorification, nevertheless, a certain understanding of their intrinsic importance is present. Granted that the very core of their nature as values is not understood, i.e., the inner nobility, the message from above which every value embodies, he still has an understanding of these values, restricted though it is; and he is also able to respond to them with a kind of admiration and respect. Yet his admiration and respect do not constitute a real value response for, despite them, his response lacks the elements of submission and reverence which are characteristic of all value responses. It is more a case of being impressed by values. But, nonetheless, his response is a positive one.

According to the depth and nature of the pride in question, there is a broad scale of variation concerning the nature of the understanding of extra-moral values and the nature of the response motivated by them. The same must be said with respect to concupiscence. What matters in our context is that we may find people who are completely blind to all morally relevant and moral values, and therefore radically indifferent toward them, and yet grasp—though in a very distorted way—the beauty of nature and art and even go off into a transport about them.

Granted that certain types of proud men have a limited understanding of some extra-moral values and others not, the question arises: What is the nature of the difference between the various types of pride—satanic, pharisaic pride, the pride of a Richard III, and the pride of a Don Giovanni? Is it a difference of degree? In all these different types, the humble, loving, reverent center is silenced; in all of them, the sphere of morality is treated disrespectfully and purposively ignored. Obviously, then, it is not a question of the degree to which pride silences the moral value-responding center, since in all of them that center has been silenced. And yet it is not wrong to say that Cain is prouder than the pharisee and the pharisee prouder than a Richard III or a Don Giovanni. In each case we are speaking truly when we mean by "prouder" that the satanically proud man is more imbued with the evil genius of pride, that he partakes to a greater extent of its very essence. Hand in hand with this "greater" pride—greater in the above-mentioned sense—goes a deeper quality of pride and a greater consistency concerning the immanent logic of pride. Thus, the pride of the satanic type is a deeper pride, a more evil, a more refined, a "purer" (i.e., more unmixed) pride.

This becomes clearer when we realize that in all the different types of proud men, apart from the satanical and the pharisee, pride is always mixed with concupiscence. In Richard III as well as in Genghis Khan or in Don Giovanni or Don Rodrigo, there is a clear interpenetration of pride and concupiscence, though with a different accentuation. In Don Giovanni and in Don Rodrigo, concupiscence is perhaps predominant; thus the interpenetration of pride and concupiscence is easily perceptible. In Genghis Khan or in Richard III, pride may prevail, but the element of concupiscence cannot be missed. In the pharisee, pride predominates completely; concupiscence may be absent, but it can also be present. In the satanically proud, on the contrary, there is no place left for concupiscence, because pride attains here a consistency and power which implies an exclusiveness. Thus we see that we have to distinguish, in regard to the morally evil man in whom the loving, reverent center is silenced, between different degrees of participation in the evil genius of pride, degrees which imply differences of quality and depth.

Blindness to moral values and outspoken antipathy to the

moral sphere are to be found in everyone whose basic attitude is dominated either by pride or by concupiscence or
by an interpenetration of both.[3] Yet the type of pride (satanical, pharisaic, etc.) has a bearing on the special nature of
moral value blindness. Above all, blindness to extra-moral
values and the relation to these extra-moral values depend
on the degree of pride, i.e., the quality and depth of pride.

By that we touch upon a very important epistemological
problem of a more general order. What is the scale in the
degrees of understanding an object? In our context, however,
it is with the scale in the degrees of grasping a value that
we must concern ourselves. Although we are led to this
epistemological problem in our present study of the proud
man's relation to extra-moral values, we shall show the
stages in the grasping of values by typical examples taken
from the realm of concupiscence.[4]

A blunt concupiscent type is unable to grasp the very
quality of purity and will never make any distinction between
an impure and a pure person. Another type, and a more
refined one—for instance, Don Giovanni—may grasp the
quality of purity in another to such an extent that it is seen
as characteristic of this other person. But it is completely
misunderstood and in no way grasped as value. In a man
it will appear to a Don Giovanni as a silly weakness, an impo-
tent effeminacy. In a woman it will attract him, but in no
way as a moral value, but as something inciting his lechery,
and as subjectively satisfying.

Unlike a Don Giovanni, an aesthete will perhaps be able
to grasp purity as a value in other persons, but still not as
a moral value. He will see it perhaps as a poetical charm, as
an aesthetic value, as something like the purity and freshness
of a landscape early in the morning, and still sparkling with

[3] The pharisee forms an exception *sui generis* in this respect. Cf. *True
Morality and Its Counterfeits*, Chapter I.
[4] We choose our examples from the realm of concupiscence because they
are particularly illustrative of this epistemological difference.

dew. He will see purity in the light of virginity, and virginity in the light of a vital and aesthetic value.

Though an aesthete already sees this datum much better than does a Don Giovanni, nevertheless he overlooks completely the very core of purity, its character of moral value. In fact, he grasps the datum of purity so vaguely that he confuses it with other data related to it, for example, virginity; and his grasp is so superficial and incomplete that he overlooks the essential character of purity as *moral* value.

Other types who are not exclusively dominated by pride and concupiscence will grasp purity as a moral value, but because of their distorted conception of the entire moral sphere, they will confuse purity with a kind of conventional "decency." Because for this type convention and morality run into each other, many single virtues are also seen more or less in a conventional light. Although purity is perceived as a moral value, insofar as the moral obligation to be pure is grasped and understood, its profundity and "mysterious" moral quality are not apprehended.

Finally, we have the morally conscious man who clearly grasps the specific quality of purity as moral value, free from any confusion with conventional "decency." Only in this case is an authentic awareness of purity attained. Yet there exist still many degrees of a deeper and more intimate understanding. A saint grasps the full intrinsic beauty and moral import of purity still more clearly than the morally conscious man. But these degrees go in another direction than the aforementioned.[5]

[5] Progress to higher levels of understanding can be referred to in three different ways. First, we have a scale reaching from complete blindness to a clear grasping of purity in its character of moral value. These stages—implying decisive differences concerning the extent to which the object is understood in its very essence—are the ones which imply an important epistemological problem. Secondly, there is the scale of degrees concerning depth and plenitude in the framework of an authentic awareness of purity as a moral value. Thirdly, there is a completely new type of progress in knowledge: the transition from immediate, naïve experience to a philosophical *prise de conscience*. This third type goes in a completely different direc-

After having barely hinted at this epistemological problem of the different stages reaching from a complete unawareness to a full value perception, we turn back to our analysis of the differences in the relation to values which we find in proud men.

Insofar as pride is in question we have the following scale of value blindness. In the satanic type we find a blindness to all values, but an awareness of their metaphysical "throne," especially the "throne" of moral values.[6] In this type we find an open war against all values as values. Yet this does not exclude the possibility that technical values such as energy, or acuteness of intellect, may be desired by the satanically proud, but only for self-adornment. As mentioned before, the satanically proud wages war, above all, on moral values; here pride displays itself not in the desire to be endowed with them for self-adornment, but rather in the attempt to dethrone them and sit on their "throne."

The pharisee also apprehends the metaphysical throne of moral values; he understands their incomparable superiority in this respect, but unlike the satanic man he wants to possess them for self-adornment; he wants to sit on their "throne" through the possession of these values.

A Don Giovanni or a Don Rodrigo type, on the contrary, comprehends many extra-moral values, though not in an adequate manner. Such a type appreciates wittiness, intelligence, courage, beauty as being precious and praiseworthy.

---

tion, for it refers to a theoretical consciousness, presupposing a philosophical eros, i.e., an interest in a thematic, systematic knowledge. The immediate awareness of purity need not necessarily be greater in the one who reaches a philosophical *prise de conscience* of the datum of value and of purity as a moral value than in one who does not. The progress of knowledge achieved in the philosophical *prise de conscience* is something *sui generis*. We can prescind in our context from this increase of knowledge. Neither is the second type of differences our topic here. It is rather the first type of scale which is illustrative of our problem, that is, the stages of value blindness in persons dominated by pride or concupiscence or by both.

[6] We have explained the nature of this metaphysical "throne" of values in *Christian Ethics*, Chapter 35, p. 443.

Thus Don Giovanni will admire them in other persons. But, surprisingly enough, he is blind not only to moral values but also to their metaphysical throne; he does not desire to possess them; he would see no glory in their possession. They are for him no source of satisfaction for his pride. He is thus even blinder to moral values than the satanically proud, Cain or Rakitin. However, he understands some extra-moral values much more than does the satanical man, insofar as he comprehends not only their "throne," but also something of their importance-in-themselves.

Yet our main topic is the man in whom a subconscious compromise is to be found between pride and concupiscence on the one hand and the loving, reverent, humble center on the other. He grasps the importance of morality as such. But because of this compromise, he will be prone to confuse such extra-moral values as courage and self-control with moral values. He will also understand certain virtues such as reliability, justice, loyalty, honesty in their character of moral values; and will desire to be endowed with them, partly from a moral point of view, partly from the point of view of pride. This man shuns the idea that he himself may be dishonest, disloyal, unreliable, or unjust. And he finds it especially unbearable to be considered so by others in his own social world. He certainly does not desire these virtues solely for the sake of sparing his pride, for he is also aware of the moral obligation to possess them. Indeed, he will even look at them primarily as something morally obligatory.

But it is extremely illustrative in our study of the formation of substitutes for morality to see which kinds of extra-moral values are attractive to pride as substitutes for the moral sphere, while embracing as substitutes all kinds of genuine moral values which on their part are also attractive to pride, because of a certain misinterpretation.

Summarizing we may say: If we prescind from satanic pride, we may distinguish the two following types of proud men: First, the man who grasps certain extra-moral values and makes an idol of them in opposing them to moral values. He has a hostile attitude toward the moral sphere as such; he is blind to it and yet opposes it; he is openly at war with morality. But he grasps, for example, the value of extra-moral courage and views even his rebellion against morality in the light of courage. Such is Don Juan in Mozart's opera, *Don Giovanni*. He could not bear to see himself in the light of a timorous person. Secondly, the man who makes of an extra-moral value (such as courage in its extra-moral form) a substitute for morality, a representative of the moral sphere. This is the compromising type. He chooses an extra-moral value which is bearable for his pride—that is, does not force pride to abdicate completely, and which is congenial to his attachment to the moral sphere.

In the realm of concupiscence we find a scale concerning the relation to extra-moral values analogous to that we found with respect to pride.[7]

The brutelike concupiscent man is too coarse to grasp beauty. He ignores the very nature of this value and perceives no difference between beautiful music and the purr of a smoothly running motor. The beauty of nature leaves him cold. The datum of beauty is thus completely overlooked.

A less brutelike concupiscent type, e.g., a Casanova or an Aristippus of Cyrene, may see the beauty of a face, and of many things in nature—a horse, for example—and he also enjoys the wittiness of a companion, but he never recognizes them as values. He never grasps the intrinsic preciousness and dignity of all values which call for an adequate response. He perceives enough in them to distinguish them from neutral and indifferent things, and to enjoy them, although certainly in a very inadequate fashion. Even certain qualities

[7] We dealt before with different stages of value blindness due to concupiscence from an epistemological point of view. It helped us to throw light on a general epistemological problem concerning stages of awareness. Here we come back to stages of value blindness due to concupiscence, from a moral point of view and with respect to the genesis of substitutes.

which are in fact moral values, for instance, friendliness, kindness, patience, are grasped and liked. But they are in no way understood as *moral* values.

Again in an aesthete, as was mentioned before, we find a greater awareness of extra-moral values; and as for aesthetic values themselves, a certain understanding of their character as values. He considers them important in themselves and precious and not merely attractive. In him aesthetic values become an idol which is opposed to morality as that which should replace it.

For our problem, however, it matters to distinguish the following two types: First, the type dominated by concupiscence who grasps certain extra-moral values and makes an idol of them in opposing them to moral values. Such a type feels resentment toward the sphere of morality and would replace the moral sphere with an extra-moral value, the way, for instance, the aesthete does with beauty. Secondly, the compromising type who makes of an extra-moral value (for instance, genuineness, being true to oneself) a substitute for morality.

Genuineness is certainly a value, but not a moral value. It is an extra-moral value which a man mainly dominated by concupiscence may grasp and appreciate. In any case, it does not hurt concupiscence as moral values do. Thus it is understandable why the compromise between concupiscence and the moral center leads to make of genuineness a substitute morality.

Moral goodness is identified with genuineness or being true to oneself; and moral evil, with "insincerity," that is, with conformity to a law imposed on us against the trend of our own personality.

The symbiosis of the moral value-responding center, on the one hand, and pride and concupiscence, on the other, displays itself here in the deformation of the moral sphere, a deformation which identifies morally good and evil with an extra-moral value and connects the most formal character of the moral law—as a binding norm for our conduct, withdrawn from our arbitrary wishes—with an extra-moral value which does not hurt our pride or our concupiscence.[8]

After having analyzed the relation between certain extra-moral values on the one hand, and pride and concupiscence on the other hand, we are able to understand better the genesis of substitute moralities. We understand how certain extra-moral values (because they are bearable for pride and concupiscence, and even attractive for them) are chosen to become exponents for morality, that is, to form a substitute morality.

What underlies this compromise is, however, no conscious choice. On the contrary, it is something infra-conscious which is taking place in the depth of our soul. The readiness to submit to the moral norm, and domination on the part of the value-responding center, is still so restricted, the concessions made to pride and concupiscence are such, that an extra-moral value which does not antagonize pride or concupiscence in a specific way becomes a denominator for the entire moral sphere. In saying "entire," we in no way mean

[8] In comparing the scale of value blindness and relative value perception in the realm of pride with that in the realm of concupiscence, we can state the following characteristic difference.

The satanically proud, i.e., the one most imbued with the spirit of pride, is less blind than the man of brutelike concupiscence. Though he also is blind to all values, he nevertheless sees their metaphysical throne and even the "unique" throne of moral values. But the brutish concupiscent man does not even grasp their metaphysical throne. He ignores the very presence of these values, regarding them torpidly, without noting whether or not they are actually present in a man.

In coming to the less radical types of pride and concupiscence (radical in the above-mentioned sense of the degree of submission to the evil genius of pride, as well as the degree of depth), we can state that the concupiscent type will be better able to have some awareness of certain values in other persons and in goods, which he himself would like to possess, than the proud type. Above all, he will be ready to assume a friendly attitude toward them. Thus, as we have seen, the aesthete is capable of grasping purity in other persons as something positive, as a value, though not as a moral value. He will also enjoy friendly and polite persons, and peaceful, unselfish people will be pleasing to him.

that *all* moral and morally relevant values and disvalues are seen and included in the moral sphere placed under the title of this extra-moral value. On the contrary, the inevitable consequence of this deformation is a segmentation of the sphere of moral and morally relevant values and disvalues, so that only one part retains a moral significance for the proud or concupiscent man while the other is reduced to something morally neutral or indifferent. In saying "entire moral sphere" we mean that the extra-moral value is identified with the genus of the morally good and functions as a general moral denominator. The deformed notion of moral sphere will always embrace some real morally relevant and moral values, but it will necessarily exclude some others from this sphere.

The substitute for morality built up will combine the following elements. First, the most formal features of the moral norm and moral theme: its objective oughtness, its character as the most central and important thing—a relation to conscience. Secondly, a deformation and perversion in introducing an extra-moral value as content instead of the real morally good and evil. Thirdly, the inclusion of some real morally relevant and moral values in this deformed notion of the moral sphere; but these are misinterpreted in view of the extra-moral value functioning as general denominator.[9] Fourthly, the ignoring of many morally relevant and moral values which are regarded as morally neutral. Fifthly, the distortion of the formal nature of the moral norm and moral sphere by the substitute. (It has still an oughtness, but this oughtness is no longer quite the authentic one; it has still a relation to conscience, but this relation is lacking in genuineness.)[10]

[9] When certain things which are really good morally are praised and others which are morally evil are condemned, we can consider such responses as coincidental, since complete moral understanding is lacking.

[10] We shall deal with the different elements of the substitutes for morality later on, as well as with these different dimensions of perversion.

We are now able to understand better the kind of compromise embodied in the substitutes. The ethos is not the one which we found in the mediocre man who shuns profound devotions and self-abandonment. Far from it, for the adherent of a substitute may prefer even to die rather than to flout the norm prescribed by the substitute. The greatest fervor and an implacable duty-ethos may be found in an adherent of a substitute. Nevertheless a compromise is in question, although it displays itself at a much deeper level and its origin goes much further back, that is, to the very process of the formation of the substitute. The very fact that a substitute exists testifies to the symbiosis of the positive and negative centers and to the presence of a compromise; and the very nature of the substitute discloses the specific nature of the compromise. Yet in order to understand the nature of the substitutes we have to take into account not only the attractiveness of certain extra-moral values for a mitigated pride and concupiscence, but also the extra-moral aspects of certain moral values, aspects which also explain why certain moral values will be included in the deformed moral sphere, and others left out.

## Chapter VII

## EXTRA-MORAL ASPECTS OF MORAL VALUES

AFTER HAVING ANALYZED the role of extra-moral values in the formation of substitutes, we have still to examine another important factor in the genesis of substitutes—the extra-moral aspects of *moral* values. They play a role especially in the case in which a single moral value is made a substitute for the entire moral sphere.[1] Surprising as it is, even moral values can be approached from an extra-moral point of view. For example, generosity possesses the character of an extra-moral superabundance, that of "breadth" and of "uninhibitedness." Thus the generous man also distinguishes himself from the avaricious and even from the parsimonious man by an element of freedom and of independence. His attitude, as opposed to narrowness and pettiness, has a liberating effect on us. The generous man also arouses admiration and love because of this "breadth." This aspect is a true efflorescence of the moral value in question. It is one essential facet of its beauty. So far we have not concerned ourselves with an extra-moral aspect. Yet when this legitimate aspect of breadth is wrongly emphasized and, as it were, isolated, leaving out all the other features of generosity and even its specific moral goodness, it assumes an illegitimate character, and is tainted with aestheticism.

It becomes fully an extra-moral aspect when it is not only isolated and wrongly emphasized, but when it is confused with an extra-moral value—the "breadth" which certain prodigal people also possess, as opposed to the narrowness of

---

[1] It is the case which is predominant in the realm of heretic substitutes.

the avaricious or parsimonious man. To view generosity in the light of a much more general breadth, a breadth which it however possesses eminently, amounts to a misunderstanding of generosity and to a falsification of it. One overlooks the specifically moral value of generosity; one reduces it to an extra-moral value, that is, to the temperamental charm which we find in prodigal men who are not simply a prey to their wishes, but who are prodigal toward themselves and toward others because of a lightheartedness and the pleasant carelessness of the *cicada* in La Fontaine's fable. Sometimes this type of prodigality is also connected with a superabundant vitality. To identify the breadth of generosity which is free from all arbitrariness with this temperamental charm, lovable as it may be, implies a blindness to the essential difference existing between both. The wideness of generosity is not a species of "wideness" considered as a genus, nor is prodigality. The "breadth" of generosity is only analogous to the "breadth" of prodigality.[2]

It is not difficult to see that this wideness, apart from its being an extra-moral value, is also something subjectively satisfying. To feel oneself wide, the opposite of petty and narrow, is a satisfaction for pride and concupiscence. The "master position" of giving, distributing, bestowing on others is likewise satisfying for pride and concupiscence.

The specific charm which this virtue conveys to a person in the eyes of others also makes it enjoyable for the bearer of this charm. It is like a beautiful garment which one likes to wear, in which one feels adorned. This "enjoying" does not have the spirit of a value response, though it presupposes the perception of the value of generosity. But interest in the possession of the charm it conveys to oneself in the eyes of

[2] There are, however, many other notions of breadth which refer to authentic values, though not to moral values. Such is, for instance, the wideness of a personality possessing a great stature. In contradistinction we find a pseudo-wideness, proper to personalities who—because of their weakness, their indiscriminate yielding, and unsubstantiality—have, as it were, no boundaries. Clearly, this is only an apparent wideness.

others has the character of an enjoyment of what is subjectively satisfying.

Thus the man unwilling to be "too hard" on his pride and concupiscence may accept generosity as a virtue, as something praiseworthy, interpreting it in the light of an extra-moral aspect which it possesses eminently.[3]

In a similar way reliability and loyalty can be appraised because of their extra-moral aspects. Reliability and loyalty convey to a person the character of "seriousness," of being a reliable member of society; in short, they endow him with a certain aureola of honorableness. This aspect is certainly not so "extra-moral" as the above-mentioned "breadth," but it is tainted with utilitarian elements. Even an amoral person will certainly prefer to have reliable employees and loyal servants, for these moral qualities also have an eminent utilitarian worth; they are needed for the functioning of community life, for attaining practical ends. This usefulness is clearly an extra-moral value. In the same way values whose extra-moral character cannot be doubted, such as alertness, intelligence, and even health, are practically useful and sometimes indispensable for the attainment of certain ends, for the fulfillment of certain tasks. An immoral man may view reliability, honesty, and loyalty in the same light as alertness, intelligence, or health, namely, as necessary presuppositions for efficiency—that is, in their extra-moral aspects.

It is easy to see that this extra-moral aspect of these moral qualities makes them attractive even to persons in whom pride and concupiscence prevail. Insofar as these qualities are embodied in other persons they may attract the immoral man on account of their usefulness, as previously mentioned. But the proud man even wants to possess these virtues for himself, because he sees them in the light of seriousness, correct-

---

[3] In saying that generosity possesses the "breadth" of the temperamental charm in an eminent fashion, we mean that the extra-moral value—that is, all that which is really good in it—is also to be found on a much higher and essentially different level in the moral "breadth" of generosity.

ness, and self-control, all of which are extra-moral values which cater to his pride.

These extra-moral aspects also play a role in building up substitutes. They facilitate the peculiar combination of extra-moral and moral elements as well as the creation of a wrong denominator for the entire moral sphere. They also explain, above all, why it is sometimes a special moral value which functions as substitute, being illegitimately identified with the general notion of morally good.

The role of extra-moral aspects of moral values refers, however, not only to the genesis of substitutes. It also displays itself in the case of less radical deformations, such as the alleged cores of morality.[4] But even this does not exhaust the role of these extra-moral aspects of moral values. For in the context of the important ethical problem of the purity of motivation, or of the pure moral value response, the question how much such extra-moral aspects interfere is of great import. Patently these extra-moral aspects are often interwoven in the motivation of moral actions, at least partially so. On the one hand, there is a certain corrosion of the moral value, at least a lessening of it. But on the other hand, the extra-moral aspect may be a most welcome support for keeping a man morally on the right track.[5]

We mentioned in Chapter III, as one of the substitutes for morality, the opposition of "noble" and "base." We find certain persons who declare that they will never do anything vile; the distinction which counts as norm for them is no longer one of morally good and morally evil, but rather the distinction of noble and vile. It is true that there are certain immoral actions which have the connotation of meanness. Meanness is a real objective quality, a special disvalue of certain immoral attitudes. But not every immoral attitude has the specific connotation of meanness. To kill someone in

[4] Cf. Chapter II, E. "Degrees of Deformation."
[5] The analysis of the role of extra-moral aspects in the moral motivation is of the greatest importance for pedagogy and spiritual direction.

a duel is not foul, but certainly it is thoroughly immoral. Whereas to betray a friend, to abuse his trust, is base. Francesca da Rimini's sin is not vile; nor is Othello's murder of Desdemona base.

Here also it is an extra-moral aspect of the moral disvalue of meanness which is the reason why one substitutes a special moral disvalue for the moral evil as such. Meanness has a specific ugliness, an element of filth, a depressing pettiness. It has a bad odor.

At first glance one might suppose that the quality of meanness indicates a specific degree of immorality, that it is equivalent to the gravity of a sin, the "rank" of a moral disvalue. But this is wrong, as we can see if we consider two well-known characters in literature, Father Karamasov and Rakitin. The former is especially vile, whereas Rakitin is not foul though in his diabolical pride he is certainly as evil if not more so. Cain is not specifically vile.

The impossibility of interpreting the qualities of "base" and "noble" as connotations of the rank of the moral disvalue or value is still more obvious if we consider the positive quality, the "noble." Certain morally good actions and attitudes have the specific connotation of being noble, for instance, generosity or forgiveness; but others, such as reliability, honesty, and humility, lack this specific character, although humility is the highest virtue apart from charity. Even in the case of martyrdom, the highest-ranking moral action, one would not call it noble. Martyrdom is above this quality, indeed it surpasses "the noble" in its sublimity to such an extent that the predicate "noble" no longer does justice to it. Thus the quality of "noble" certainly is not a mark of the rank of the moral value.

On the other hand, some things which are only moral imperfections and which imply no moral guilt in the strict sense may still have a connotation of meanness. The following story may illustrate the "meanness" of a morally harmless deed. Two gentlemen dine in a restaurant. Upon leaving the table, one of them gives a tip of ten cents; the other gives only five cents. But before the waiter arrives to pick up the tip, the latter quickly pushes the two tips together, in order to give the impression that he was as generous as the other person. He clearly wants to combine a petty saving with making a good impression.

Obviously, this action is not a crime. It does not imply a moral guilt, although it certainly betrays a certain moral baseness. It is a base action and is more the opposite of nobility than Othello's murder of Desdemona, though the latter implies a heavy moral guilt and is definitely a grave and terrible sin. In the case of the man who replaces morally good and evil by "noble" and "base," an extra-moral aspect of moral values and disvalues creeps in, and it is this extra-moral aspect which appeals to pride and concupiscence.

Just as there are certain moral failures which shame us more than others, so certain moral disvalues hurt our self-esteem more than others; they are more likely to be sources of inferiority complexes. To approach moral values and disvalues from the point of view of self-esteem or an inferiority complex is equivalent to being motivated by an extra-moral aspect of moral values. Such an approach still involves a moral sense, a perception of certain moral values and an interest in them. But on the other hand, it is an approach which is dictated by extra-moral norms. The character which undermines self-esteem and fosters inferiority complexes is not restricted to moral failures, but is also connected with many extra-moral disvalues—lack of courage, letting oneself be abused by others, being forced to swallow humiliations, a display of intellectual inferiority; in short, all the things by which, as the Italians say, we make *brutta figura* have this depressive character, which has, as such, always an extra-moral aspect, even when it is rooted in moral disvalues.

There is a fundamental and essential difference between contrition and the depression caused by a moral failure. Contrition is a pure moral value response, a condemnation of one's sin because it offends God, a turning away from it because of its moral disvalue, its intrinsic incompatibility with God, the Eternal Judge.[6]

The depression which one feels because one has been abased, or because one feels miserable, or because one has an antipathy toward oneself, is no *moral* value response, in fact no pure value response at all. Yet in the frame of natural morality, it is not illegitimate, for it has its root in the legitimate interest in a great objective good for the person, namely, that one should not feel oneself abased, that one should be able to esteem oneself and correspond to a pleasing image of oneself.

But this interest definitely differs, even in the frame of natural morality, from the specifically moral attitude. The fact that this image of oneself also embraces extra-moral values and that the depressing experience of inferiority can be a result of extra-moral disvalues, as well as of certain moral disvalues, clearly proves the extra-moral character of the quality of baseness or of nobility. They are seen in the light of the general aspects of attractiveness, calling for respect or the avoidance of *brutta figura*. And, furthermore, this interest in being attractive to oneself, and in being able to esteem oneself, does not have the character of a pure value response, but rather of a mere "liking."

As soon as these extra-moral aspects of moral values play a preponderant role in our motivation, a grave moral deformation takes place. It may lead us to identify certain moral values

---

[6] In contrition we find a unique relation to the very "genius" and nerve of morality as such. The man who experiences real contrition places himself, as it were, in the very axis of morality; he responds out of its "logos"; he embodies it. In condemning his own fault, in revoking it, he emancipates himself from his own person and stands, as it were, on the side of the moral norm; he approaches it from the love of God. Here we touch on one of the elements which determine the overwhelming moral value of contrition.

Even the imperfect contrition in which the fear of punishment predominates is focused on God.

and disvalues, such as noble and foul, with morally good and evil.

This selection among moral values, which ignores many other moral values and restricts morality arbitrarily, is determined by the preponderant interest in the extra-moral aspect of moral values. This aspect which appeals to pride and concupiscence is made the representative of morality as such. The compromise which takes place is here especially obvious because one makes a real moral value the denominator of all morality—a value which simultaneously also appeals to pride. It is not only bearable for pride, but even satisfies a mitigated pride because of its extra-moral aspect which it shares with many extra-moral values.

Thus we see the role played by an extra-moral value in the case where "noble" and "foul" in their opposition become either a substitute morality or an alleged core of morality. To be "base" is depressing for our self-esteem, it has a character of "foulness" which makes us particularly ashamed and miserable.

We mentioned previously altruism, warmth of heart, duty as heretic substitutes for morality.[7] Here, as in the case of "noble" and "base," a special moral value has illegitimately become the representative of all morality. Yet these substitutes are not only rooted in an extra-moral aspect of the respective moral value, as in the case of "noble" and "foul." Thus when the morally good is considered to be equivalent to "altruism," what we have is not so much a morality rooted in an extra-moral aspect of this moral value, but rather a morality poisoned by pride.

It is also true that altruism—an active concern with the welfare of others—has an extra-moral aspect, namely, that of efficiency. The altruist regards himself as efficient, in contradistinction to those for whom their *own* happiness, their *own* perfection play a role. And he feels efficient especially when

[7] Cf. Chapter IV.

he compares himself with those in whose lives contemplation occupies an important place. He contrasts his efficiency with the "waste of time," the egoistic inertia of others, and he is contemptuous of contemplative monasteries.

Efficiency is clearly attractive to pride, and so is the element of practical productivity. Thus here these extra-moral aspects of altruism also play a role in the genesis of this substitute. But the main element is another one. It is the antithetical character of this substitute, the protest full of indignation against other people, which is the key to an understanding of this substitute. This protest full of indignation is a typical satisfaction of pride. It is linked to an element of self-righteousness.[8] One feels morally superior with respect to "selfish" people. The aggressive character of this morality, its defamation of all legitimate interest in one's own objective good as selfish, clearly reveals this element of self-righteousness. The symptoms of pride are to be found equally in the "hardness" which this morality shares with all antithetical and aggressive moralities. This deformation of morality is not characterized by an extra-moral aspect, but rather by the very poisoning of morality by pride.

The "moral" character, the moral point of view, is especially stressed here; and the deformation, instead of being an aestheticism, or a deformation resulting from an extra-moral aspect which has crept in, is a narrow, moralistic one. The role of pride is here more direct, without the detour through an extra-moral aspect of a moral value, a detour which still implies a reference to an extra-moral value. The sphere of extra-moral values is not involved here, except for the aspect of efficiency. What we have here is a deformation of morality in the very frame of morality itself by pride. It is the type of deformation which puts moralism in the place of morality, falsifying morality by narrowing it, hardening it, poisoning it with self-righteousness.[9]

[8] Cf. *True Morality and Its Counterfeits*, Chapter II.
[9] Cf. *True Morality and Its Counterfeits*, Chapter II.

There are, however, different brands of altruism as substitute morality. Apart from this aggressive type which we dealt with, there is also a humanitarian, soft type, the philanthropist who theoretically identifies morality with altruism, who declares, "What could morality be except to help our fellow-men, to make them happy?" [10]

Here the stress is not laid on action alone, nor has it the self-righteous, acid taint. It is rather a sentimental, soft, emasculated morality. It appears in many different nuances and shapes, from a Herbert of Shaftesbury down to the specific elimination of all morality concerning our direct relation to God. It overlooks morality in its relation to our self. It reduces everything to sympathy with other persons and to interest in their happiness.[11] The soft, sentimental philanthropist tainted with a crass rationalism and with utilitarianism is often more concerned with an abstract love of humanity than with deeds helping one's neighbor. These types either write about altruism or content themselves in becoming members of philanthropic associations.

In these cases of altruism the influence of pride and concupiscence manifests itself in the watering down of morality to a sentimental philanthropism—that is, to a morality deprived of all metaphysical depth, of the "breath of eternity." Such philanthropists already find a satisfaction of concupiscence in their own jolly mood. They live in an atmosphere breathing a certain epicurean spirit, and the substitute of altruism is a projection of this ethos. The reduction of morality to a social affair makes it bearable for pride and even attractive for concupiscence. A sentimental softness satisfies a certain type of concupiscence, and the detachment of moral-

[10] It must, however, be emphasized that some humanitarians were really men of good will who did much to wipe out judicial torture, terrible prison abuses, and many other evils. In spite of their philosophy and their ethos, they have the incontestable merit of introducing in the institutional field many things which in fact are practical consequences of the Christian spirit.

[11] Certainly the above-mentioned aggressive type may also be found in the frame of humanitarianism.

ity from God and from religion is clearly a concession to pride.

Moreover, altruism has also the aspect of conveying to a man the character of being a useful member of society.

We have mentioned in Chapter III that even "duty" can become a substitute morality and an alleged core of morality. In this case, duty is equivalent to everything which in a tangible way has been accepted as a task, for example, the fulfillment of a promise or the discharge of an office to which one has been appointed, or the exigencies of a position or function—in short, all kinds of moral obligations which in one way or another have also a juridical aspect. Morality is here restricted to a kind of reliability and a spirit of responsibility; but it leaves out goodness, a spirit of forgiveness, generosity, and many other prominent moral values. In fact it formalizes and sterilizes the wealth and plenitude of moral values and reduces all morality to faithfulness and responsibility in the fulfillment of all things to which one has been assigned or which one has freely accepted. To forgive an offender, to help one's neighbor or to have compassion, to rejoice over the conversion of a sinner, is not a "duty" because no task which has been accepted is in question.

Thus to make of duty, in this sense, the denominator of all morality is to exclude the core of morality and to condense all morality into the accomplishment of all exigencies required by the specific nature of a task and its immanent logic. This perversion is characterized by rigidity and dryness and by a military ethos, and is thus deprived of all the splendor and irresistible beauty of true morality. Dutifulness tends also to glide into an ideal of extra-moral usefulness and of efficiency, embellished with the social image of the man whom one can take seriously, on whom one can rely—the good worker, the loyal citizen, and so on.

The substitute of duty in this sense played a great role in the Prussian mentality, especially in military circles. The mixture of a formal specifically moral notion with an extra-moral juridical element also has its roots in the extra-moral aspects of this "dutifulness" and in the appeal of this extra-moral aspect to a certain pride.

We encounter here a certain paradox: on the one hand, a spirit of correct submission to authorities, and formal superiors; on the other hand, a spirit of pulling oneself up, holding one's head upright, feeling oneself "high" and strong.

The dutiful man in this sense is also attractive to a bureaucratic mentality which considers all other moral commandments as vague and as issuing from a kind of romantic idealism. The dutiful man in this sense is endowed with a social respectability which is not exclusively due to his real moral merits, but to his usefulness and smartness. The reliability proper to the dutiful man is indeed a great advantage for community life.

Here we have also to distinguish two relations to pride: the extra-moral aspect and the direct corrosion by pride. The fulfillment of a tangible, clear-cut task appeals to pride, for reliability has, as we saw before, an extra-moral aspect which is attractive to it. To fulfill everything to the brim which one has accepted is a source of self-assertion and a satisfaction of pride. In this context it possesses also an affinity to efficiency which is, as such, an extra-moral value and one which clearly appeals to pride. Thus in this notion of duty also, we easily see the role played by an extra-moral aspect of a moral value. But that which, above all, reveals the role of pride is the reduction of morality to this fulfillment of tasks, a reduction which lends itself to a juridical formulation. The ostracizing of love in morality, the despising of all moral values which do not fit into this duty scheme, reveals an element of hardness and self-assertion which is a clear outgrowth of pride.

As we saw before, yet another notion of "duty" can assume sometimes the character of a substitute or of an alleged core of morality. We are thinking of people who identify morality with hardship, with doing something in spite of the fact that one dislikes it, that it is done *à contre coeur*, that it is repulsive to one's nature. The man who acts with moral rightness out of a superabundant love of God, whose heart burns to do so, who rejoices in performing a morally good action, has for them no moral merit; as a matter of fact, he seems to them to be morally insignificant. Here again we find two elements in which the role of pride displays itself: first, an extra-moral aspect and secondly, the direct corrosion of morality by pride.

As regards the first, duty is seen in the light of self-control, energy, virility, mastery over our heart. These people do not admire a dutiful man because his will is so strongly devoted to the morally relevant good that despite the reluctance of his nature and even of his heart, he conforms to it, but simply because he disregards his nature and his heart. The hardship which has only a moral significance as a test of the degree of devotion and abandonment of the value-responding will is admired and praised for its own sake.[12] The value of being able to endure hardships, to act against our nature, and to dominate ourselves is patently an extra-moral value and one which appeals in a specific way to pride.

But the second factor, the direct corrosion of morality by pride, is even more important. It results in a kind of hatred of pleasure, happiness and delight of all kinds, a hatred which is a specific form of pride, i.e., a gnostic pride filled with mistrust and hatred on the part of a pervert moral zeal directed against every delight and all forms of the *delectabile*.

In this peculiar form of pride, which is mixed with moral elements and a fanatic zeal, the satisfaction of pride displays itself, in a hard, puritan virility and in a *ressentiment* against the light and harmony embodied in the delightful.

[12] Hardship may have a high moral significance when it is a test of the degree of devotion and abandonment of the value-responding will. The fact that someone is ready to do something morally good even when he must accept great sacrifices in order to accomplish this deed is certainly a proof of the degree of his interest in the morally relevant good. But apart from its function as a test for the degree of interest, the hardship implied in a sacrifice is also a specific actualization of this unlimited abandonment, ultimately of his love of God.

Cf. Dietrich von Hildebrand, *In Defense of Purity* (New York: Sheed & Ward, 1935); *Christian Ethics.*

Here again, just as in the case of altruism, we face a specific moralism, a caricature of the moral sphere rather than a confusion of the moral sphere and the extra-moral one. Here again there is a direct influence of pride, again there is the connotation of self-righteousness, and again a hardness and moral acidity.

In the Tolstoian "warmth of heart," a real moral value is grasped. "Warmth of heart" appeals to the moral value-responding center. Here the moral value which is made a substitute for morality is also sought from the moral point of view. Yet the fact that it is made a substitute morality clearly reveals the role of an extra-moral aspect of the eminently moral value of "warmth of heart." It is confused with the extra-moral value of *human,* genuine, affective, in contradistinction to the cool, reasonable, and voluntaristic. Charity is wrongly seen in the light of the mere warmth and genuineness of a sensitive heart.

But here also the intervention of pride displays itself primarily in the antithetical character of other moral values. However, we do not find self-righteous pride which we detected in the above-mentioned heretic substitutes. What satisfies pride here is the ousting of moral norms, and of anything lawful which is imposed on man. It is not self-righteousness, but rather the tendency to see every submission to a law, all morality connected with juridical liabilities, every formal morality, even every reasonability as tainted with self-righteousness.[18] The role of pride displays itself here in the revolt against any moral authority. But this revolt appeals also to concupiscence. The cult of genuineness, of impulsive reactions, does away precisely with the obstacles to concupiscence. Perhaps the appeal to concupiscence is in this case even stronger than the appeal to pride. In saying that the only

[18] That the adherents of this substitute may also fall into a kind of self-righteousness was shown in the discussion of those who fight against pharisaism and mediocrity in *True Morality and Its Counterfeits,* Chapter VIII, "Sin Mysticism."

thing which counts is "warmth of heart," the burdensome yoke of moral laws, which concupiscence shirks, is thrown off.

Moreover, the cult of impulsiveness also has in itself a relation to self-indulgence. Not only do the ostracizing of laws and rules imposed on us and the defamation of reason as cold and self-righteous betray the role of concupiscence; but the cult of impulsiveness likewise betrays the relishing of a kind of unchecked effusion of our feelings.

We now also see the difference in the genesis of naïve and heretic substitutes. In the naïve substitute, the role of pride and concupiscence manifests itself mainly in the confusion of moral and extra-moral values, in making a qualitatively extra-moral value the formal denominator of morality. In the heretic substitute, the influence of pride and concupiscence comes to the fore, on the one hand, in the role of the extra-moral aspect of moral values; and on the other, in the role of the antithesis to other moral values, an antithesis which in certain cases may assume the character of a sour moralism, a caricature of true morality.

## Chapter VIII

# FORMAL EXTRA-MORAL NORMS

WE DISTINGUISHED IN Chapter III between formal and material or qualitative substitutes. We mentioned tradition, state laws, and progressiveness as examples of formal substitutes. Now we shall analyze two of them, the cult of tradition and the cult of state laws, in order to elaborate first their extra-moral character, as such, their relation to morality, and finally their relation to pride and concupiscence.

Tradition has, patently, such a broad scope and is a datum of such fundamental importance that we do not intend to offer a complete analysis of it in this frame. We restrict ourselves to an elaboration of the features of tradition which have a bearing on our problem of substitute morality.

For many people tradition is the norm which imposes moral obligations on them and to which they are willing to conform. What tradition prescribes is for them morally right, what tradition prohibits is for them morally wrong.

Before discussing the value of tradition and its extra-moral character, we must briefly delineate the nature of tradition. We must, however, emphasize from the very beginning that there exists an essential difference between human tradition and the sacred, divine tradition of Holy Church. After having sketched the nature of natural or human tradition, we shall point out the nature of sacred tradition and its difference from the human one.

In its widest sense tradition embraces the entire heritage of former generations. It presupposes the possibility of personal intercourse, of communication from one person to another. But it refers to the communication from an older to a younger

generation, and not to the interpersonal communication between persons of one and the same generation. It refers to the
process of spiritual heritage, to receiving what former generations deliver to us. Tradition in this sense is actualized in
the relation of parents to their children; it actualizes itself in
any form of education; in the influence exercised by a nation
on the individual growing up in it; it manifests itself in every
idiom; it is at the basis of any cultural development.

Tradition is the spiritual stream flowing from one generation to another, gushing forth in each new generation, being
eventually enriched by it, flowing on to the next generation.
Without tradition, there would obviously be no history.

But the nature of tradition implies a lived heritage. Books
in which important insights are objectivated and which
through this formulation and objectivation make these insights accessible to further generations are not necessarily
parts of tradition. They are rather potential instruments for
tradition. Only when they play a vital role in the generations
immediately following them—such as, for instance, in an ex-
ceptional way, St. Augustine's *De Civitate Dei* in the early
Middle Ages—do books have the character of elements of
tradition.

Tradition is thus, in its most formal character, a spiritual
stream flowing from one generation to another and embracing
all domains of life: the domain of knowledge, of convictions,
of principles; the domain of moral attitudes, the cultural
domain, as well as the domain of civilization.

Tradition in this sense plays a role in small communities
as well as in large ones; it functions as an instrument in local
communities as well as in the entire history of mankind.

Yet we have to distinguish between the objective fact of
tradition and the tradition which is, as such, consciously experienced. We could term the first "objective tradition" and
the second "subjective or conscious tradition." The first is
the objective dimension of communion, embodying the element of continuity in the community. It is the channel which

enables a living heritage to flow from one generation to the following. In this wider meaning of tradition, consciousness of the process of inheriting plays no role. To what extent the one who inherits something knows that he received it from a former generation is not decisive. What matters is that, *de facto*, he did inherit it. Yet it has to be objectively inherited in such a way that it really continues to live in the younger generation.

The narrower sense of tradition, on the contrary, implies a consciousness of the process of inheritance—that is to say, the inherited contents are labeled as "inherited." It implies that one feels oneself to be standing in the stream of tradition, that one is aware of this living link with former generations. Obviously, subjective tradition always presupposes objective tradition. We are here concerned with the subjective or conscious tradition, since it is only tradition in this sense which can become a substitute morality.

Subjective tradition implies, however, a specific intention on the part of the *majores* (forefathers) who transmit the spiritual heritage to the following generations. It is the intention of transmitting something precious, a treasure which is entrusted to the younger generations. Tradition claims to be the transmission of the "sanctuary" of a community, the treasure which gives the community its meaning and dignity.

On the part of the heir it is equally received as something precious, delivered up to him to be highly esteemed and cherished. Here the specific nature of tradition discloses itself. Something which survives in a new generation merely by habit is by no means a part of tradition. Neither a completely indifferent practice nor still less a bad habit resulting from self-indulgence (and experienced and deplored as bad) can ever claim the honorable title of tradition, even if it subsists in later generations in the way of an inherited disease.[1]

Whatever may be, objectively, the value of the content of

[1] It would plainly contradict the true meaning of tradition to speak of the tradition of getting drunk or of gambling in a family.

a tradition, tradition implies by its very nature a reference to a precious heritage, precious by its nature, because it has been cherished by ancestors, and because of its character as a "sanctuary" around which the members of the respective community are gathered. The tradition of a family, of a tribe, of a nation refers always to the "name" in which the members of the respective community are gathered together. The "name" to which we refer here is not the realm of goods which is the "theme" of a family in contradistinction to a state or to a religious order. We mean here by "name" the theme which varies according to the individual family, or individual nation, and thus distinguishes one individual family or nation from another. The tradition of such a community rather refers to the "name" in which the members of one individual family, one individual tribe, one individual nation are gathered together. It refers to this secondary theme which is their individual specialty. This formal feature of tradition by which it claims in some way to be a "sacred" heritage is of the greatest importance. Here we find the starting point for making of tradition a substitute morality.

It is, however, necessary to understand that tradition implies two elements: stress on the preciousness of the content of the heritage and stress on the preciousness which results from its character as heritage, that is, from the role which it plays as "sanctuary" of an individual community. Both titles of preciousness are interwoven in the subjective tradition. But the emphasis laid on either one of these two titles may greatly vary.

In the case in which tradition refers to a treasure of truth (scientific, philosophical, or religious),[2] or when it refers to moral principles, the stress may be laid entirely on the preciousness which the content possesses as such. Tradition

[2] We are not thinking here of the supernatural tradition of Holy Church with which we shall deal later on. We are thinking of a human tradition concerning religion, such as in Buddhism, Islamism, or, as in the family, tradition concerning the Christian religion.

could have a serving character whereby the entire emphasis is placed on the truth of the conviction and the validity of the moral principles and not on the fact that they are a part of tradition. In this case tradition adds nothing to the content which speaks for itself. Here tradition is in no way thematic, and its relation to a moral principle or to truth is not affected by the question whether a mere objective tradition is at stake or a subjective conscious tradition.

But it may be that a certain emphasis is also laid on the second title of preciousness. The fact that former generations held something as true, and adhered to it, may imply a kind of recommendation. It may imply an appeal to consider it with a certain reverence, at least with a friendly disposition.

But this "recommendation" does not yet have any weight as an argument for the truth or validity of the content. Tradition still has a serving character; it recommends only, but it does not arrogate to itself the role of an argument. It adds to the truth and validity of the content an element of venerability, as a treasure revered and cherished by former and venerated generations.

Natural tradition should never go further and offer itself as an argument for the truth of a proposition or the moral value of an attitude. In doing so tradition assumes an illegitimate role, and the danger arises that it may become a channel for error, superstition, and moral blindness. It is precisely in this role that it also can become a substitute morality. We shall thus come back to this illegitimate role of tradition. Before discussing it, we must, however, first distinguish other functions of tradition.

The content of a tradition implies, apart from the universal elements (the truth of a proposition or of a moral principle), the specific individual manner and way of the respective community. If we think of the tradition of a nation, we have to distinguish between, on one hand, the insights acquired by a nation and its discoveries (the truth of which is, by its very nature, universal) and on the other, the individual features, e.g., the ethos, the type of spirituality and intelligence it possesses.

Insofar as tradition refers to the way in which a truth is formulated—the style of thought, the specific talents, the individual features of an ethos, the type of humor—in short, insofar as tradition refers to all these individual traits of a nation, the emphasis on the heritage as heritage is naturally greater. It is here that the notion of "our tradition" assumes its specific meaning. The individuality is experienced in a specific way as a distinctive character of the respective community. In this atmosphere created by its individuality, the members feel at home, and experience their belonging to this community. Thus it is the heritage of this collective individuality which is primarily considered as a specific possession of this community (which belongs to them) and which gives to tradition the character of being "ours."

The above-mentioned gesture of delivering something precious is, however, not restricted to individual features, but embraces also that which is considered to be an important truth or a moral value. Yet the attitude toward the universal elements differs from that toward the individual elements, so long as tradition remains in its legitimate frame. With respect to the individual elements, the fact that they are part of tradition plays legitimately a greater role. Here the value of venerability deriving from the heritage as heritage, or from the fact of being cherished by the *majores*, may legitimately be more emphasized. Likewise, the element of belonging to "our" tradition legitimately comes more to the foreground.

These features belonging to the individual character express themselves in a specific way in customs, styles of life, ways of life, institutions.

Here tradition may surpass the objective fact of heritage and recommendation and the element of a certain venerability. Whereas in the case of truth and morality, the superimposed value of venerability which principles receive by tradition is incomparable in weight with the truth or the moral value itself, in the case of customs, institutions, forms of life, the value superimposed by tradition may be even more important. Thus tradition may even become legitimately a reason for preserving certain customs and institutions. Yet this applies only in cases in which customs, institutions, ways of life have no definite disvalue. If they embody a disvalue, it is clear that this disvalue would turn the scale with respect to the superimposed value of the traditional.

As mentioned above, we have to distinguish clearly between the human tradition and the sacred, divine tradition of the Church. After having dealt with the nature of human tradition in a wider and narrower sense, we want now to point out briefly the nature of sacred tradition and its difference from natural tradition.

The tradition of the Church claims to be based on divine revelation.[8] By this fact tradition assumes a completely different character. The revelation of the Old Testament and the self-revelation of God in Christ are unique, and the stream of divine truth and divine life (in the Sacraments) has been entrusted to a community.[4] Tradition assumes thus in the *Corpus Christi Mysticum* the character of a supernatural reality; the historical tradition is here only the natural basis for the continuation in time of the stream of divine truth and divine life. Here the fact that the content of a dogma is part of the tradition is the all-important argument for its truth. In a field in which the truth is inaccessible to our reason, in which Revelation alone can convey it to us, and in which faith

[8] We are not concerned here with the question whether the claim of Holy Church to embody a divine tradition is true or not. This is a question of faith. But the difference between the nature of the tradition which the Church claims to embody and all types of human or natural tradition can be grasped by our reason, and is a topic of philosophy. Thus in expounding briefly the difference between the two types of tradition, we in no way quit the realm of philosophical knowledge and enter into that of theology.

[4] In the official language of the Church, one distinguishes between *traditio* and *scripturae*. Our context does not require an analysis of this difference.

reigns instead of knowledge, no intrinsic evidence or proofs of reason can carry the point. The very fact that it corresponds to Revelation is the decisive question, a conformity which, precisely, only the living tradition can guarantee. Thus we are confronted with a situation which is the pure reverse of the one in the realm of natural tradition. If a man gives as argument for a natural truth which can be grasped by our reason that it is part of a tradition, plainly this argument is philosophically invalid.[5] The tradition is here no guarantee for truth, whereas in the case of dogma the only decisive argument is that it is part of the tradition. Thus this sacred supernatural tradition differs here in a twofold manner from the human tradition.

First, it is part of the continuing stream of divine life and lies under the protection of the infallible magistery of the Holy Ghost. The *successio apostolica* exhibits the continuity of this holy tradition and the essential character which it has here.

Secondly, appertaining to this tradition is the very guarantee of being part of the Revelation, and thus the fact that something is part of tradition and that it had always been embraced by the faith of the Church is *the* argument for its truth.[6]

To confuse these two notions of tradition—the human, natural and the sacred—would be a disastrous error. To make of the sacred tradition a mere human tradition and to look at it with a respect motivated by the venerableness which any old cultural tradition possesses is in truth a radical misunderstanding of the holy tradition. To say, be faithful to the faith of your fathers, is equivalent to replacing the question of truth by a mere faithfulness to a venerable tradition, and is

[5] St. Thomas: *"Auctoritas est locus ultimus in questionibus philosophiae."*
[6] In order to belong to revealed truth, the only requirement is that a dogma was in fact implicitly included in the faith of the apostles. It is not necessary either that it be explicitly implied or that there be a document proving the presence of this article of faith in the historical tradition of the apostles.

just the opposite of a recourse to the holy tradition of the Church, which would be the very emphasis on the question of truth.

Clearly, Holy Church, being divine and human, possesses— apart from the substantial sacred supernatural tradition—also a merely natural historical tradition. This applies to certain customs, secondary elements of the liturgy, and organizational rules. This tradition is certainly more venerable than any other because of its intimate union with Holy Tradition, but it differs radically from it, being a historical human tradition. Elements of this tradition have been given up and replaced by others. Conservative as Holy Church is in this respect, there have been changes according to the historical circumstances, just as, analogously, there have been changes in Canon Law. This tradition makes something venerable, but it can never be compared to the Holy Tradition, which belongs to the very core of Holy Church as a divine institution.

In turning back to our topic, human tradition, we must now examine its value. Tradition in the wider sense has undoubtedly a high value. First, it has an indirect value as an indispensable presupposition for culture. The high good which culture and civilization embody is not possible without tradition. If every generation had to start *ab ovo*, neither culture nor civilization would ever come into existence. The very existence of families, as we saw, implies an element of tradition in education; and, patently, a nation presupposes tradition, a tradition reaching through many generations. Language is already a product of tradition, and vice versa. Likewise, history itself in the full sense of the word would not exist without a link between different generations.

The indirect value of objective tradition as an indispensable presupposition and a means for culture, for science and civilization, and indeed for any progress and development, is so obvious that we need not insist on it.

But objective tradition has also a direct value. It is, as we saw, a fundamental element of community; we could say, a fundamental dimension of community. We mean here the very dimension of community and the specific type of communion which is embodied in tradition, in the handing over of so many things, in the link between generations, in short, what we called the continuity dimension of communion. As such it partakes of the intrinsic value of communion and community, which we have discussed in another work.[7]

Objective tradition, or tradition in the wider sense, has thus a definite value of its own. This value is a formal one. If the content of a tradition is evil, it would certainly be better if this tradition did not exist. The question of the content of tradition is always the decisive one. Patently, the indirect value of tradition will be turned into an indirect disvalue when the content of the tradition is either morally evil or is marked by errors, superstitions, and false religions. The direct value of tradition, on the other hand, will be overshadowed by the disvalue of its content.

We turn now to tradition in the narrower sense, i.e., subjective tradition, which is our concern in this context. Granted that the content of tradition is a positive one, tradition—as we saw before—still adds an element of venerableness to the good possessing an authentic value.

The fact that a good endowed with an authentic value is old, that it comes to us through the ages, that it has existed throughout a long period of history, subsisting through various cultures, undoubtedly conveys to this good a value of its own. A beautiful church built eight hundred years ago has, apart from its beauty, a venerability through its age.[8] It is the

---

[7] Cf. Dietrich von Hildebrand, *Metaphysik der Gemeinschaft* (Regensburg: Habbel, 1955), Section 4.

[8] We are not speaking of the advantage which a Romanesque church possesses if built in 1100 in contradistinction to a Romanesque church which has been built today, even if both were absolutely identical. This advantage is based not so much on the venerability through age, but rather on the fact that the earlier church is an authentic objectivation of the mentality of the twelfth century, whereas the new one built today is a

entire rhythm of history which manifests itself here, and the specific character which this rhythm conveys to something which has subsisted through historical periods. By age we are referring not to the purely objective duration, for instance, the age of a metal hidden in the mountains. We have in mind an age which involves insertion in the rhythm of history.[9]

From the venerability which something possesses because of its historic age we must distinguish the venerability deriving from tradition. The value of "traditional" is rooted in the respect and veneration felt for former generations. The fact that they cherished and cultivated certain principles gives to these principles a certain aureola. The respect for one's own ancestors and the recommendation acquired by the fact that cherished principles have stood the test of time, and of the community from which one stems, convey on them this aureola.

Yet we must still distinguish between the venerability deriving from tradition and that deriving from age as such. The venerability stemming from a subjective tradition always implies that the tradition is ours. As there are different cultures, so there are different traditions. The venerability which something received by tradition applies only to elements of the tradition which is our own. It is attached only to certain goods for those people to whose tradition these goods belong. The

---

copy. Had the contemporaries of Fischer von Erlach compared his Karlskirche with the Gothic church of Maria Stiegen, the argument in favor of the authenticity of the older church would be groundless. As both are equally beautiful, the older one does not possess the advantage of originality, because the new one is also an original and in no way a copy.

This value of authenticity and originality, which enhances greatly the aesthetic value, must be clearly distinguished from the value which old age and tradition as such convey to something.

[9] This venerability of historical age corresponds to the venerability of age in an individual. An old man calls for respect. In former times this was clearly understood as is evident in the notion of "senate" (assembly of old, experienced men, having acquired wisdom through the plenitude of their experience, from their having lived through different periods). In our present epoch the cult of the young tends to overshadow this deeply human respect for the aged.

venerability on account of age, on the contrary, is not restricted to elements of one's own tradition.

The character of traditional endows a truth or a principle with the character of something tested by time, something analogous to the weight deriving from the *consensus multorum* or *omnium* (the agreement of the many) or from the *communis opinio*.

We mentioned before that this venerability plays legitimately even a greater role when tradition refers to customs, institutions, or ways of life. Yet it is clear that the value of tradition, as such, has never the character of a morally relevant norm. To observe a tradition is morally good when the content of the tradition is morally relevant, but never merely because something is part of a tradition. Every element of a tradition which contradicts truth or the moral law must be abandoned from the moral point of view. And the fact that something belongs to tradition, though being in no way indifferent, never constitutes a morally relevant good, and still less can it impose moral obligations on us.

Nevertheless, the fact that something is an element of tradition has often been dealt with as if it were a source of moral obligation; to give up a tradition is in many cases considered as a kind of infidelity, nay, even a treason. Yet tradition as such, apart from its content, in no way imposes upon us the moral duty of faithfulness.

There is, however, a virtue which, though having a wider range than the realm of tradition, is also a value response to tradition, a response given to the dignity and venerability which something possesses as an element of tradition, as something respected and loved by our ancestors or by the generations preceding us. This virtue is a specific form of reverence related to filial respect, for which the German language has coined a specific term: *Pietät*.[10]

[10] There exists no English word which adequately renders the meaning of the German term *Pietät*. We shall therefore use the German word. Its specific meaning will become clear from the context.

*Pietät* is certainly a virtue including moral values. Undoubtedly, the elements of reverence and of faithfulness which this virtue possesses are positively good from a moral point of view. This virtue is, however, not only to be found as a response to tradition. In order to understand the specific nature of *Pietät* we shall first try to sketch its nature in general.

The most typical element of *Pietät* is the respect for things past. A man shows *Pietät* if he deals in a respectful manner with a friendship which, for certain reasons, has ceased. The fact that it meant much to him in the past calls for holding "high" the memory of his former friend and that of their friendship, and not for simply laying it aside, because it did not last. Again, a man manifests *Pietät* when he respects the intentions of his dead father or of a dead friend or of a dead master. The fact that a certain action is not according to the spirit or intention of his father or mother who are both dead is, for him, a reason for omitting something which he would like to do. Though it does not hurt the person who has passed on to eternity, though he knows that he cannot make this person suffer as he might if he were still alive, he still honors and respects the person's intention, as, for instance, the intention of a deceased author concerning the interpretation of his work.

We prescind here from the case in which these wishes or intentions refer to a morally relevant good, that is, from the case in which their fulfillment is morally obligatory because of their content and not because of the deceased person's intention. We also prescind from things which we are compelled to fulfill because of a formal obligation, such as, for instance, a last will and testament.

*Pietät* implies respect for the intention of those gone or absent as well as for our past experiences, and for customs and habits sanctioned by tradition. It includes elements of reverence, faithfulness, and continuity; and its general characteristic is the relation to the past. A thing does not lose its claim to be respected and held in a respectful memory merely because it belongs to the past, considered in one sense or another. On the contrary, *Pietät* is even increased by the fact that something is no longer present, as when, for example, an author can no longer defend his intentions from being abused or disregarded, because a relation imposing observance and respect as a matter of course no longer subsists. It is a kind of special generosity toward the "unprotectedness," the weak position of things past.

After having dealt with *Pietät* in general, we now must study the role of *Pietät* with respect to tradition. *Pietät* is also a response to the value which something assumes because of tradition. Here it is less the forementioned "generosity" than a certain awe, an elementary respect for the pregiven frame of life, the things lovingly delivered up to us by other generations. Here the element of faithfulness mixed with gratitude prevails.

*Pietät,* in this sense, is thus a response to the abovementioned character of a "sanctuary" which is handed over by the *majores.* We stressed before the solemn gesture by which the content of tradition is delivered. We could express it in the words: "Here is the treasure we confide to you; honor it, be faithful to it." *Pietät* is the response to this gesture; love and gratitude for one's ancestors call for this reverence toward things considered by them high and precious. *Pietät* toward the traditional is also a response to the solidarity with the world from which one stems, from which one has received so much, to which one is so deeply indebted. Thus we see that a response to the value of tradition also includes moral elements. Undoubtedly, *Pietät* is a noble attitude.

However, the virtue of *Pietät* is not, as such, obligatory, although it implies moral elements. To a certain extent, it may be obligatory, insofar as it refers to persons, parents, ancestors, and so on; and insofar as the elements of faithfulness, gratitude, and love are concerned. A certain disposition to listen attentively may perhaps be morally obligatory, as when we find it worth while to examine seriously certain convictions and principles handed over by tradition, or when we approach them with a certain reverence, so long as they are not clearly recognized as evil or false. But never is it morally obligatory to cling to them only because they are part of tradition; on the contrary, it is strictly obligatory to discard any conviction or principle as soon as we have definitely grasped its falsity. It may even be morally required to reject emphatically a tradition whose content is morally evil, or pure superstition. Here also the words of St. Augustine apply: "Kill the error, love the one erring."

In turning to the different forms in which tradition can assume an illegitimate role, we must distinguish among the following steps of deformation leading to tradition as substitute morality.

The first consists in the fact that one considers the venerableness of traditional things—which, as such, are morally neutral—as imposing on us a moral obligation to cling to them; one believes, for instance, that he is morally obliged to cling to certain customs or institutions exclusively because they are traditional. One would feel unfaithful, irreverent, in short, morally guilty, were one to give up traditional customs or habits either because he dislikes them or considers them superannuated or because a certain situation calls for giving them up.

In this case tradition is not yet a substitute for morality. It still leaves open the possibility that moral principles and morally relevant values are grasped in their independence from tradition. The error consists only in interpreting tradition as a morally obligatory reason for clinging to things which are morally neutral. It consists in making of the venerableness of the traditional a source of obligation, at least so long as it does not refer to morally objectionable things.

A second step of deformation consists in considering faithfulness to tradition not only morally obligatory, but even the highest moral obligation. Here one does not yet confuse morality with tradition, but one believes that faithfulness and loyalty to tradition impose the moral obligation to cling to an institution or custom even when it is considered unjust or morally bad. Here faithfulness, *Pietät*, overrules all other moral obligations. We find this attitude often in persons who —while interiorly converted to the truth of Catholicism— shrink from entering the Church because they do not want to be unfaithful to the religion of their fathers. They really believe—paradoxical as it may be—that in doing so they would become guilty of unfaithfulness, of a kind of treason. In short, they make of unfaithfulness to tradition a morally insurmountable obstacle.[11]

A third step of deformation is reached when morality and tradition have become coextensive. This "identification" may, however, have different reasons.

It may be that tradition assumes the character of a theoretical authority.[12] The judgment of the *majores*, the fact that the traditional views of the community in which one feels imbedded have been tested through the generations, has a theoretical weight which one does not dare contradict. Whatever one's impression may be concerning a traditional principle, rule, or institution, one does not believe oneself competent to oppose the traditional opinion. Yet, actually, one conforms to tradition because of the conviction that tradition is the best guarantee for the truth and value of the principle in question. Thus one admits a *moral* obligation rooted in morally relevant values, and one only submits to tradition because it is taken as a theoretical authority and as the most competent judge about what is right and wrong.

---

[11] The conflict between the "duty" to be faithful to tradition and the obligation to follow the voice of one's conscience has been the topic of many novels and dramas.

[12] Cf. Dietrich von Hildebrand, "Das Wesen der echten Autorität," *Menschheit am Scheideweg* (Regensburg: Habbel, 1954), pp. 341-407.

A much more radical identification of morality with tradition is to be found in the case in which tradition does not function as theoretical authority but as the formal source itself of moral obligation. Here one confuses *Pietät* with the basic *religio*, that is, with the fundamental bond of submission to God and to the moral norm. One identifies the dignity and venerableness of tradition with the majesty of the moral law. Thus what has been handed over by tradition is regarded as true, good, and even morally obligatory.

Here tradition has become a substitute morality. What is morally good has not only become coextensive with the content of one's tradition, but the fact that something is part of tradition is regarded as the very source of its moral relevance. Here *Pietät* has become a substitute for morally good, and the lack of *Pietät* is identified with morally evil. However, the formal *eidos* of the moral sphere, its majestic obligation, its appeal to our conscience are attributed to tradition. Loyalty to tradition is here adorned with the ultimate seriousness and obligatory character of morality. A link to morality is thus definitely still present.

We shall understand this type of substitute better if we realize that it has the character of a kind of infantilism. For a small child it is normal that commands and prohibitions of his parents are more or less synonymous with morally good and morally evil. The parents are representative of the moral sphere; they are the moral authority, to obey them is equivalent to being on the right moral path.

It is the normal process of growing into adulthood that the young person distinguishes more and more between the moral sphere, and its obligations, and the respect due to parents. Normally, the adult clearly distinguishes between obedience to the moral law and conforming to the morally relevant goods on the one hand, and *Pietät* toward parents on the other. In the case in which tradition becomes a substitute, this essential distinction has not been made. The moral authority of the parents is transferred to tradition, instead of being replaced by the moral sphere. The parental authority is extended to one's ancestors, to the tradition of the tribe, the people, or the nation.

In the more primitive form there is a specific deformation of reverence. The "pregivenness" of the human ground on which our existence is built up (our parents, our ancestors), and with it the whole inherited world of convictions, habits, and customs, is confused with the autonomous objectivity of truth and the moral law. The reverence due to the sphere of morality, ultimately to God, is thus erroneously applied to the venerableness of the traditional, which calls, as we saw, for a completely different kind of reverence. The confusion is analogous to the case in which the cult of ancestors replaces religion, or in which our ancestors assume the role of God.

The degree of moral deformation obviously depends to a great extent upon the very content of a tradition. If tradition were, in its content, in full conformity with the authentic moral sphere, the deformation would be much less than in cases in which a tradition recommends morally wrong things or at least tolerates them, as in the case of material substitutes such as honor. But the substitute morality which may be the content of a tradition is not our concern at the moment. If a tradition implies the duty of "blood revenge," this immoral heritage is a material deformation which must be distinguished from the formal substitute of tradition as such. But apart from any eventual material deformation in the equation of tradition with morality, a formal deformation would be present, even if the content of the tradition were blameless. The real majesty of the moral sphere, its breath of eternity, is replaced by a merely human venerableness. And this implies that not even a single moral and morally relevant value is really understood.

Something should be done, it is said, because tradition tells us so. Here moral precepts are not only exclusively known in the frame of tradition, but the moral obligation is confused with the "sacredness" of tradition. The majesty and incomparable seriousness and categorical imposition of morality are erroneously believed to be rooted in tradition. The formal moral *eidos* is still seen but is erroneously ascribed to tradition. In the case in which tradition is seen in its relative character, and morality is consciously reduced to this tradition, tradition is then no longer a substitute for morality, but an amoral idol, such as in the conception of a Charles Maurras or of a relativist aesthete.

The confusion of *Pietät* with the basic *religio* corresponds to the confusion, on the object side, of the merely formal character of being commanded (positive commandment) with the moral value (moral commandment); and also to the confusion of the character of being commanded by God with the venerableness of tradition.

Yet here, as always, to confuse two things can still have very different meanings. There is a decisive and essential difference according to the direction of the equation which is at the basis of this confusion. It has often been stressed how very different it is whether someone equates God with the world or the world with God. In *Christian Ethics,* we pointed out the abyss which separates the conception of Aristippus, who equates value with the subjectively satisfying, from that of Max Scheler, who considers the subjectively satisfying to be a lower type of value.[13] In our context we have to emphasize the difference between equating morality with tradition and equating tradition with morality.

In the latter case, tradition is erroneously made the source

---

[13] Yet, needless to say, even the more favorable equation which raises lower to higher entails an error with respect to the higher. Apart from implying a grave error with respect to the nature of the lower element which is equated with the higher, it also bars the adequate understanding of the higher.

In equating the world with God, one not only misinterprets the world, but the notion of God is also necessarily affected by this equation. In making of the merely subjectively satisfying a value, we necessarily falsify also the notion of value. It belongs to the full understanding of the value that we grasp its essential difference from the merely subjectively satisfying. This applies to all illegitimate equations.

of morality and it is thus adorned with certain formal features of morality. Tradition "obliges"; it appeals to one's conscience; to disobey it makes one feel guilty; it possesses the formal character of a moral norm. This is the case in which tradition is a formal substitute for morality. In the former case, in which morality is identified with tradition, tradition is no longer a real substitute morality. It amounts, on the contrary, to a reduction of morality to something extra-moral, or to our stripping morality of its absolute character. It is a dethronement of morality instead of a substitute morality.

In the case in which tradition is a substitute morality, tradition appears, as it were, in the garments of the moral sphere. Tradition is illegitimately elevated to the rank of source of moral obligations. In the case in which morality is reduced to tradition (with tradition regarded in its relative character), morality is clothed in the vestments of tradition, or, as we can say, morality is degraded to the level of tradition.

We have just said that the identification of morality with tradition is not a substitute morality. However, we must qualify this by saying that there are different degrees, or stages, of confusion or equation of morality with tradition. Even when morality is equated with tradition it can still have the character of a substitute morality, so long as tradition is not understood in its relative and human character.[14]

We cannot enter here into an analysis of all the different nuances in this frame. We must restrict ourselves to stating the two different directions of the equation, while stressing, moreover, the frame in which tradition can still have the character of a substitute morality, and beyond which the equation would assume the character of an amoral idol, as in the case of Charles Maurras.

In saying that in tradition as substitute morality certain formal features of morality are still to be found, we must,

---

[14] In the case of the *Action Française,* for example, Charles Maurras reduces religion to a human tradition which he sees in its relative character, though overrating its value.

however, understand that the equation of tradition with morality inevitably corrodes the formal *eidos* of the moral sphere. Though the moral sphere still has the character of a supreme norm or moral obligation, it no longer has the character of a "breath of eternity," the authentic majesty of the true moral sphere. It is leveled down inevitably. This is the case with every formal substitute as well as with every idol. In making an absolute of something which is not absolute, this pseudo-absolute can never have the same absoluteness as the true absolute, even concerning its formal character; one can never place a usurper on the throne of the legitimate king without the throne itself undergoing inevitably a desubstantialization.

Has this extra-moral norm of tradition any relation to pride and concupiscence analogous to that between them and such extra-moral personal values as self-control, energy, courage? In general we could say that tradition is rather repulsive to the concupiscent man who regards as undesirable every limitation placed on his search for pleasure.

But, on the other hand, the confusion of *Pietät* with *religio* is a specific symptom of moral primitivism, of an incapacity for grasping the true nature of morality. And this moral primitivism is due to concupiscence.[15] The moral commandments are not clearly distinguished from traditional customs or conventions. It is, furthermore, a kind of infantilism in which the merely positive commandment and prohibition are not yet clearly distinguished from moral commandments; and it is from concupiscence that this lack of wakefulness stems.[16]

Again we may say that the proud man is averse to tradition,

[15] A certain laziness underlies the tendency to cling to the familiar and to shun the new to which one is not accustomed. To adhere to tradition, insofar as it coincides with the opinions, ways of life, customs, moral principles to which one is accustomed, can thus also be a result of spiritual laziness, which again is rooted in concupiscence.

[16] In the small child this confusion is natural and faultless. In the adult the analogous confusion is morally faulty and is due to concupiscence.

because he shuns the acknowledgment of any bond; and thus we find it typical of a certain pride to rebel against tradition. In a very typical way an adolescent wants to break with tradition. This childish pride aims at the independence which consists in throwing off tradition.

Yet the ethos of the type of substitute morality in which faithfulness to tradition is placed over all other moral obligations, and is even identified with faithfulness to God, has, indubitably, elements of pride and concupiscence. This faithfulness appeals to self-esteem, it gives us the impression of being firm and stable; it nourishes a self-image which is attractive to us. It is perhaps most visible in the case of the man who is aware of the immorality of some elements of his tradition, but believes that faithfulness to tradition overrules any other moral consideration. Here one places consistency, faithfulness to an image of oneself, above fidelity to God. It is similar to the case in which one makes of consistency a moral idol, or in which one believes that keeping a promise must be preferred to any other urgent moral call.[17]

In this perversion, there is always an element of pride—the disproportionate role of faithfulness to oneself, a preference for being sheltered on the safe ground of a self-assertion instead of following God's call as embedded in morally relevant values. Formal correctness, or consistency, or fidelity to one's word sustains this self-assertion.

Nationalism and class conceit, whether of aristocrats, bourgeois, or workers, imply a clinging to tradition. The pride which is at the bottom of nationalism and of class conceit is a motive for being faithful to tradition. Let us not forget that tradition is in all these cases experienced as one's own tradition. One prides oneself on one's tradition; one is a part of it; it is also an enlargement of one's own person. Faithfulness to one's tradition is also a self-assertion; and pride, patently, has

---

[17] We have dealt in another book with the moral perversion which respects only formal obligations, or at least places them above all material obligations. Cf. *True Morality and Its Counterfeits*, Chapter V.

its part to play in the identification of tradition with morality. "We" and "our" are the key words of the traditionalists.

Thus we see the intervention of pride and concupiscence in making of tradition a substitute morality. It is again a compromise between the moral value-responding center and pride and concupiscence. The substitute of tradition, on the one hand, embodies elements of reverence, *Pietät*, and the admission of a moral norm; on the other, it partly satisfies pride and concupiscence and is more bearable for pride, because of the above-mentioned motives.

We now have to analyze another widespread formal substitute morality: the laws of the state in which one lives. For many people, state laws, their prohibitions and commandments, form a substitute morality.

The state has, patently, a high value. Apart from its indispensability and its character of a high good for the individual person, it is an embodiment of order and of the sphere of right and of justice. Moreover, its authority is God-given.[18] State authority is a legitimate norm in its proper frame. State laws should be respected so long as they have no immoral character, or so long as they do not pass beyond the sphere of competency of the state authority.[19]

[18] The value of the state has been expounded in detail in *Metaphysik der Gemeinschaft*.

[19] What is usually stressed is the fact that a state law imposing something immoral loses thereby every obligatory character and that we are morally obliged to disregard it. Yet it must also be emphasized that every state law exceeding the competency of the state authority can claim no obligatory character, even if its content is in no way immoral.

The grave immorality of totalitarianism consists precisely in the fact that the state arrogates rights over the individual which in fact it does not possess to itself. To impose by state laws things which are not Caesar's, but God's, for instance (to offer purely imaginary, even outlandish examples), that we be pure in our thoughts, be charitable to other persons, would obviously be a totalitarian procedure; the state would have no real authority to impose them, no right to do so, and the citizen no obligation to conform to them. The same applies to totalitarian laws which prescribe laughter at certain things, or crying, or enjoyment of a work of art.

Without raising the question whether or not state commandments imply a moral obligation, that is, whether or not
morally speaking they call for obedience, we can clearly see
that state authority and moral law can in no way be identified.
Even if someone held that it is morally obligatory to obey
state laws, these laws would, in any case, be but *one* morally
relevant good among many others, and they would certainly
be surpassed in rank by many other morally relevant goods.
To identify morality with state laws, to confuse the moral
oughtness and the majestic dignity of the moral sphere with
the authority of the state, is clearly an egregious error.

Instead of *Pietät,* as in the case of tradition, one makes of
"loyalty" the basic virtue which absorbs the entire realm of
morality. To be loyal to the state authority and to the laws
of the state is made equivalent to being a "just" man, a
morally conscientious, morally correct person.[20] The border
line of state laws is regarded as coinciding with the border
line of moral relevance.

The error which is here in question is also due to the fact
that in penal law we indeed find an important relation between state law and morality. The state punishes crimes and
in doing so acts also in the name of morality. Certainly punishment by the state is not yet the authentic response of the
moral authority to sin. This response is to be found only in
the punishment by God. Punishment by the state authority,
although objectively valid only in the name of God, is not the
response of the moral authority. Moreover, by its very essence
it extends only to the part of morality which is simultaneously
an indispensable basis for the flourishing of the state, and for
the protection of the goods which are the very theme of the

[20] The opposite of the adherents of this loyalty idol are the anarchists.
They see in any intervention on the part of the state something outrageous,
and to them the voice of morality is definitely opposed to state law. To
ignore state laws, to seek to establish justice without appealing to the state
or expecting its intervention, to act without any restriction resulting from
loyalty to the state, is precisely what is considered to be morally right and
noble.

state. In order to be a crime in the sense given by state law, an action must possess other marks besides those which make it morally evil or a sin. It must, for instance, be an injury to the rights of other persons, an aggression against public order and public security.

Thus many immoral actions, not to speak of immoral attitudes, are of no concern to the state and it would be a grave abuse for the state to make them an object of penal law. Charity, humility, piety, and meekness are beyond the concern of the state. Lack of charity, pride, religious indifference do not possess the characteristic which calls for intervention and punishment by the state. Yet, notwithstanding all these restrictions, one cannot deny that there is a relation between morality and penal law. The immorality of crimes, the responsibility for them remain essential factors in the penal law. The moral sphere overlaps the sphere of the state.

This relation between the state and morality in the penal law is one reason why the state law lends itself to becoming a substitute morality. But the error of identifying the state authority with the moral sphere is no less grave.

Again we must distinguish among the following stages of confusion between morality and state law. Someone is aware of the authentic moral sphere, but he is prone to see all the prohibitions and commandments of the state too much in the light of moral commandments. He includes within the sphere of morality things which have no moral character, just because they are proscribed or prescribed by a state law. His error consists in giving state laws a moral weight and dignity which in fact they do not possess. He has the tendency to place commandments of the state on one and the same level with the moral commandments.

But this is not yet the case in which state law assumes the full character of a substitute morality. This happens when a second stage of confusion of both spheres is reached. It is to be found in the man who really identifies moral obligation with being commanded by state authority. The formal *eidos* of the moral sphere is really identified with being imposed by state authority. They are no longer distinguished from each other and, consequently, the realm of morality and the realm of law, especially penal law, become coextensive. Moral seriousness, full moral relevance, is regarded as present only in a thing which is incorporated in a state law. Here state law has assumed the character of a substitute for morality.

Here again, as in the case of tradition, we must distinguish between the two possible directions of the equation: equating state authority with morality and vice versa, equating morality with state authority. In the former case, one overrates to an excessive degree the rank of the state and the nature of its authority; one clothes state authority in the vestments of morality, one attributes to it the formal features of the moral sphere; one sets state laws on the throne of morality. Grave as this error is—for it implies not only an undue exaltation of the state, but also, inevitably, a distortion of the notion of morality—a link with morality is still present. This is the typical case of making the state a substitute morality.

Yet, as we have said, it may also be that the equation goes in the reverse direction. Morality is identified with state laws. Morality is lowered to the level of state authority, the moral law to the level of state law. The restriction of the moral sphere, due to the identification of morality with state law, is the same as in the case of the equation of state law with moral law. In both cases, only those moral commandments and prohibitions are admitted which are simultaneously imposed by state laws. And, in both cases, things which are in fact morally irrelevant are considered as morally relevant, because they are the objects of a state law or prescription.

But in the latter equation, that which identifies morality with state law, the corruption goes much further, for it affects not only morality in its entirety, but also every single commandment or moral value. The latter equation deprives morality of its truly absolute character, of its character as the "breath of the eternal"; it is, specifically, a secularization of morality, a wrong interpretation of the formal features of its *eidos.*[21]

Even in this case, however, the notion of a norm above man, appealing to our conscience and calling for obedience, is still present, although vaguely. Thus here also state law is still a substitute. Whereas, as soon as morality is by principle reduced to a law of the state, and the law of the state is itself seen as something conventional, state law has no longer the character of a substitute. We are then confronted with a relativistic denial of morality, such as in the case of the French sociological school.

We must now pose the question: What is the relation between this extra-moral norm and pride and concupiscence?

The satanically proud is patently not impressed by state authority. He regards as hateful any authority as well as any law imposed on him. The same applies *mutatis mutandis* to the brutelike concupiscent type. He admits no norm whatever, and any law or restriction imposed on him is nothing for him but a disturbing, molesting obstacle.

Even for the type in whom a mixture of pride and concupiscence dominates, as in the Master of Ballantrae[22] or Steerforth,[23] loyalty to state laws is in no way attractive. He will disregard these laws as soon as they stand in his way and hinder his satisfaction. Yet even here an apparent conformity with state laws, the social image of being a decent citizen, is attractive to him. Steerforth does not want to be looked upon as a thief or a criminal. Don Giovanni commits crimes, but his pride interprets them in a way which allows him to regard himself as a loyal citizen who is beyond reproach. But it is

[21] The idolization of the state, called statolatry, need not always have the character of a substitute morality. It is even mostly an anti-moral idol, such as in Nazi Germany or Soviet Russia, where the moral sphere is not only pushed aside (as in the case of the aesthete's amoral idol), but the absolute authority of the state, deprived of all its original and authentic values, has a character which is hostile to morality.

[22] The main character in R. L. Stevenson's novel of the same name.

[23] One of the main characters in Dickens's *David Copperfield.*

mainly a more mitigated pride, the pride of the compromise type, which relishes the consciousness of being a loyal citizen, a decent man.[24]

It is conformity with the visible authority of the state, the social image of loyalty and decency (as opposed to the hoodlum and the rascal), which satisfies pride. Equally, the feeling of being sheltered within the state, of being on the "legitimate" side, through loyalty, is a source of satisfaction for pride. One shares, as it were, in the entire honorableness of the legitimate authority. Moreover, obedience to a state law in no way requires the same reverence and value-responding submission which are proper to obedience to the moral law, and especially to one's obedience to God. The state law does not challenge pride the way the moral law does. The submission of the adherents of this substitute morality is thus deprived of true humility. Nonetheless, their submission bestows on them a feeling of exaltation which is a caricature of the glorious exaltation resulting from true self-humiliation: *"Qui se humiliat, exaltabitur"* (He who humbles himself will be exalted). They feel that in their submission they participate in the dignity of the state, seen as an embodiment of right and justice.

To interpret the moral law in the light of a law of the state is therefore an immunization of oneself from the moral law. This makes it much more acceptable to pride and more bearable. In doing so, one deprives morality of its ultimate metaphysical seriousness and of its fathomless depth. One drags morality down to a bourgeois level, thus escaping the real confrontation with the moral sphere without losing the consciousness of being a decent man.

Finally, it is easy to understand why this substitute morality is also more acceptable to concupiscence than the true moral law. It is true that the state law imposes many restrictions on

---

[24] It is not the much deeper pride of the Pharisee, who wants to glorify himself in his moral perfection before God. It is a much more pedestrian and "modest" pride, which finds satisfaction in the social image of a decent man.

concupiscence, especially with respect to our neighbor's property. In demanding honesty within the appropriate juridical sphere, and punishing larceny and dishonest actions, it sets brakes to concupiscence.

But, on the other hand, the loyal citizen who boasts of his decency and correctness, and who never comes in conflict with the state law, still has innumerable outlets for concupiscence. Undisturbed by state laws, he may indulge in many actions and attitudes which the moral law condemns. And apart from that, this substitute morality is more acceptable because the challenge to concupiscence is incomparably weaker. The condemnation of concupiscence is not only restricted to certain crimes, but the confrontation with the ultimate seriousness and majesty of the moral law is a greater scandal for concupiscence than submission to the state law.[25]

The analysis of the genesis of these two widespread formal substitute moralities—tradition and state laws—has helped us to dig deeper into the formal *eidos* of the moral sphere. It has served to "unmask" these substitute moralities and, simultaneously, to elaborate further the difference between the moral and the extra-moral spheres.

Yet before turning to the analysis of the evil which substitute moralities embody and the relative value which they nevertheless possess as compared with amoral or anti-moral idols, we must still enter into an analysis of one of the most widespread substitute moralities: honor.

[25] But clearly this applies only to certain forms of concupiscence. As we have seen in the preceding chapter, the bohemian has a specific aversion to state laws, and would rather submit to the call of a morally relevant good. His aversion to all laws, to anything imposed on him, culminates in a hatred for state laws. And we saw before that this aversion is also rooted in pride and concupiscence. The same applies *mutatis mutandis* to the anarchist.

CHAPTER IX

# HONOR

WE HAVE OFTEN mentioned "honor" as one of the most typical substitute moralities. Because this substitute morality is perhaps, apart from the cult of tradition, most widespread, we shall delve into it more minutely. This analysis will also serve to deepen our understanding of the nature of substitutes in general.

The first problem which imposes itself concerns the question whether or not honor is a mere fiction. Does honor have a meaning of its own, or is it only an inadequate name for morality, or is it altogether a fiction, a superstition, a mere convention?

The answer must be that honor definitely has a meaning of its own, and is neither a fiction nor a mere convention. Real meaning is involved when someone speaks of his honor, although very often one labels things which have a merely fictitious relation to honor as honorable or dishonorable. It is a kind of emblem or shield which has an inside and an outside—the inner side is vulnerable to a man's own actions and attitudes, while the other side is vulnerable to the attitudes and actions of others. It is an aureola which reflects a person's status from the point of view of meriting his own esteem and the esteem of the society in which he lives. It is a kind of objective mirroring of a person's status, which indicates whether his actions and attitudes are such that he can feel himself worthy of esteem.

Two features of honor have to be stressed here. First, it is not a mere image of one's own person, nor is it the image which others have of oneself—an image which, in either case, exists only in the mind. It is an objective shield, and the question concerning the honor of someone can be answered independently of this image. Someone may erroneously consider himself despicable, although his honor is actually in no way stained, and vice versa. Secondly, the worthiness of a certain self-esteem and the esteem of others which is essential for honor is restricted to a certain type of values. Intellectual disvalues do not stain one's honor, nor do certain vital values, even though both disvalues are typical sources of inferiority complexes. To be poorly endowed intellectually is for many a source of shame, causing them to feel depressed and inferior, because they make *brutta figura* before other people.

Objectively wrong as these reactions are, it is psychologically understandable that someone who is very poorly endowed intellectually feels inferior in the presence of brilliant persons. But if he believes his honor to be stained because of this inferiority, it is not only an objectively wrong reaction but even, from a psychological point of view, one that is completely distorted. We clearly grasp that such a man lacks a clear notion of the nature of honor. The same applies to physical disabilities or aesthetic disvalues. To be crippled or strikingly ugly or extremely fat very often causes one to feel uneasy, inferior, and ashamed. But none of these conditions have anything to do with honor. The realm of honor, its most general character and meaning, is alien to these values and disvalues. We must thus clearly distinguish between honor and having a positive image of oneself.

But it would also be wrong to believe that honor is co-extensive with morality and that only moral disvalues can stain our honor. It is true that there is always a certain relation between the moral sphere and honor. We can see that by comparing honor with fame. Fame is not more related to moral values than to extra-moral values. The specific sources of fame are great deeds of heroes, great manifestations of courage, energy, and intelligence. It certainly is as congenial to great inventions, great works of art and science or philosophy as to moral values.

The fame or glory of a man does not necessarily imply that his honor is unstained. We are not thinking of a negative fame, the fame of a Herostrat, the fame of a man who, instead of gaining fame by great deeds or extraordinary talents, has become famous through his crimes, through the grave historical consequences of his failures, through the sufferings inflicted on many people. In this negative sense of Herostrat, Hitler is famous. Such fame never implies glory. We are thinking not of these but of really great men who deserve to be famous because of their great accomplishments or gifts; for example, Alexander the Great, Caesar, Napoleon, or Phidias, Titian, or Goethe, in whom fame and glory are both to be found. Yet the glory and fame which nobody will deny to Napoleon, or to Louis XI of France, or to Frederic II of Prussia, do not imply that their honor is unstained. The difference between honor on the one hand, and fame and glory on the other, discloses itself clearly. Whereas fame and glory do not necessarily imply the presence of moral values, whereas they do not have any relation to the moral sphere, honor always exhibits a certain relation to it.

But notwithstanding a certain affinity between honor and morality, honor is in no way synonymous with moral integrity. There are, definitely, moral disvalues which do not stain honor, whereas others do. In speaking of others, we may say they have sinned, but they are not dishonored or dishonorable. Othello's murder of Desdemona is a terrible sin, but it does not specifically stain his honor. Certainly we are reluctant to admit that the honor of a man is not stained by an immoral deed. And this reluctance is in a certain way justified, because honor includes a pretension to reflect moral integrity. It implies the pretension to be the emblem and shield of moral integrity, the aureola of moral integrity, the mirror of *moral* blamelessness. This claim is a wrong one, a mere pretension, because, as we have said, the true datum of honor does not coincide with moral integrity. If one tries to grasp the true character of honor, its specific quality, one has to admit that it is definitely not coextensive with moral integrity, although it implies the pretension to be so.

If, on the other hand, one takes the pretension seriously, one is compelled to say that the real honor of a man is stained by every moral disvalue, and exclusively by such. But then one has given up the original meaning and phenomenon of honor, and has identified it with something incomparably higher, to which the name of honor could be applied only in a faint analogy. Either we have to use honor in an analogous sense in which it has lost all its original character and flavor, or we have to realize the illegitimate character of the pretension associated with honor, and the difference between honor and the mirroring of moral integrity.

In this context we are interested in the nature of honor in its original character, and not in an analogous conception of honor. It is this notion of honor which is made a substitute morality. This honor is something quite distinct from moral integrity; and if we take it in its true meaning, it is correct to say that some moral misdeeds stain honor, while others do not. In this sense, honor can also be injured by other people. It implies the illegitimate pretension to be more than it is in fact, namely, to be a mirror of moral integrity. This pretension also implies an appeal that others take honor very seriously; it calls for their co-operation in abiding by the rules of the game. For honor always has a relation to one's social image. It is essentially a shield for self-esteem and the esteem of others. Thus, a social connotation is always present. Yet a further analysis of this pretension of honor discloses that its claim to be the mirror of moral integrity boils down to the claim to be the mirror of the integrity which really counts—the integrity which is decisive for self-esteem and the esteem of others. It certainly always implies a relation to morality, as we saw before; but this relation is vague, indistinct, and does not mean that the integrity in question is a purely moral one.

Perhaps the most decisive characteristic is that honor implies no relation to God. It is not concerned with the image of one's person as God sees it; it has nothing to do with the question whether or not our attitude has offended Him.

In the fact that this shield is exclusively related to self-esteem and to the esteem of others, the gap between honor and moral integrity discloses itself overwhelmingly. Moral integrity is essentially related to God; it depends exclusively on what we are in the eyes of God. This relation between moral integrity and God is an objective reality, independent of whether or not one knows of God's existence.[1]

Honor has meaning only in time, none in eternity. It is essentially temporal. This unmetaphysical and nonreligious character of honor, its essentially and exclusively intra-human, social character, discloses again the illegitimate importance which honor claims to possess. This does not mean, however, that a man believing in God might not care about his honor and that the measure of that honor might not play a great role in his life.[2] But even then it will remain something clearly separated from the commandments of God and man's desire to obey God. Characteristically enough, if he has done something morally wrong, which is simultaneously dishonorable, he will seek the pardon of God for his sin, but he will not consider the blot on his honor to be thereby dissolved. Stained honor is either irreparably stained, or it can be cleansed only by the man himself. Moreover, if he breaks through to a real contrition, he will consider this spot on his honor as a well-deserved evil.

[1] Cf. *Christian Ethics,* Chapter 36, p. 455 ff.
[2] Honor may play a great role in the life of a faithful Catholic, but we are not saying that this role is justified and is consistent with his character as a Christian. We only want to say that, in fact, honor may play a role in the life of someone who believes himself to be a faithful Catholic; and history proves that it has played a great role in some countries and in certain epochs among Christians.

The irreproachable shield of honor is in fact an objective good for the person. To be able to consider this emblem and shield of one's person as bright and shining, inside and outside, is an objective good for the person.[3] In the frame of natural morality, it is not illegitimate to be interested in this objective good which permits man to walk upright through life. It is, however, illegitimate and inadequate if one approaches a moral fault which also happens to be dishonorable from this point of view. One should avoid all moral evil because it is morally evil and offends God, without reference to his honor. But insofar as one avoids dishonorable things which are not immoral, the reference to this shield of honor is not illegitimate. The same applies to one's interest in the outside of this shield, in the fact that it has not been attacked or clouded, or spotted with dirt. Good reputation is an objective good for the person, as much so as not being treated as an underdog, or not being ridiculed publicly.[4]

Without being tautological, we have said that in the frame of natural morality it is legitimate to have this objective good for the person, because the very fact that it is an objective good for the person implies that an interest in it is at least morally unobjectionable.

We have, however, to go further and state that to be indifferent to this objective good may sometimes be deplorable, even from a moral point of view. We are thinking of people who do not care a whit about their honor, because they are either too lazy or because they are thinking only of their profit. They are willing to let themselves be treated disgrace-

[3] This character of an objective good for the person, which is proper to honor, manifests itself also in the fact that the state protects honor, just as it protects property or other objective goods for the person against injuries, although within strictly prescribed limits.

[4] We do not include here "being honored," because this refers to another notion of the term honor. The brightness of the shield of honor does not require that we are honored expressly. An honorable treatment suffices. Later on we shall deal with the notion of honor implied in the express honoring of someone.

fully if it serves their profit. Such a type is, for instance, Lebedeff in Dostoevski's novel, *The Idiot*.

These people lack dignity and are base, although in this case they are not necessarily immoral. In the frame of natural morality, their attitude cannot be called immoral in the strict sense of the term. It is unnecessary to stress that in speaking in this context of a loss of honor or of a stain on one's honor, we include only cases in which the source of dishonor is not an immoral action. We have mentioned above that in cases in which the dishonorable coincides with what is immoral, the immoral action should be avoided, not from the point of view of dishonor, but from the point of view of its immorality.

That the baseness which lack of concern for one's honor may imply is not strictly immoral reveals itself if we compare a man who shows disrespect for another's honor with a man who does not care for his own honor for the sake of his profit. Someone who would inflict on other persons the kind of treatment which affects their honor, in order to gain money or an influential position, clearly commits an immoral action. Such an action implies manifestly a lack of charity, an injury inflicted on another, the neglect of a morally relevant value, for the sake of something subjectively satisfying. It is the univocal case of an immoral action.

This is definitely not so in the case where a man neglects his own honor in order to make a profit. On the other hand, allowing our honor to be spotted is worse than sacrificing certain other objective goods for the person, e.g., the possession of material goods. A man who sacrifices a good position offered to him or a profitable transaction because he is too lazy, or because it would disturb him in the pursuit of his hobbies, is morally much less objectionable in the frame of natural morality than the man who accepts dishonorable treatment for the sake of profit.

Honor thus belongs among the objective goods for the person, and we should appreciate it. A certain moral disvalue or imperfection is therefore present in cases in which we

ignore or neglect it in order to obtain something merely subjectively satisfying or even a lower objective good for the
person.

But, on the other hand, it is morally good if we accept the
loss of this objective good for the sake of a morally relevant
good, for instance, in order to help another person. It is even
a sign of moral superiority if we are willing to sacrifice this
objective good, our honor, for a higher objective good for
the person, for instance, if someone allows himself to be
treated ignominiously by the father of a beloved person for
the sake of the high good of a marriage with her.

Later we shall see what the essential Christian attitude
toward honor should be. For the moment it suffices to see
that in the frame of natural morality the interest in this good
is morally unobjectionable, and that there exist two possibil-
ities from the moral point of view: the "dishonorable" man
who places himself beneath the level of his "honor" and the
man who surpasses this level, and whose sacrifice of this good
reveals a moral superiority, a true freedom of spirit.

In *Christian Ethics*, we distinguished between contrition,
which is concerned with moral evil insofar as it offends God,
and sorrow, which is concerned with action insofar as it is a
wrong inflicted on another person. We have already mentioned that honor has no intrinsic relation to God. Clearly,
therefore, between contrition and shame at having stained
our honor there yawns an unbridgeable gulf. Yet the shame
at having stained our honor radically differs not only from
contrition, but also from one's sorrow at having wronged
another person. We also want to stress that in the case in
which a dishonorable action includes a wrong inflicted on
another person (for instance, the betrayal of a friend, the
abuse of his trust), shame at having done something dishonorable clearly differs from the deep sorrow at having inflicted
a wrong on a friend. Out of this sorrow grows organically the
desire to beg forgiveness for the wrong done. But contrari-
wise, the shame at having stained one's own honor does not

incite one to ask for forgiveness, because even if it were obtained, the spot on one's own honor would not be removed. On the contrary, in begging for forgiveness, one accepts the spot on the shield of his honor as a deserved humiliation.

Thus we see again that this shield of honor has no relation to charity; it has no more relation to love of neighbor than to love of God. Honor is, on the one hand, a specific good for us, something essentially directed to our ego; and, on the other, something to a certain extent conventional. This does not mean that it is a pure convention, an artificial or arbitrary procedure—as when we measure distance by meters or yards and temperature by Centigrade or Fahrenheit. In calling it in some way conventional, we refer to its relation to society, or, more strictly speaking, to one's social image, its specifically unmetaphysical connotation.

There exist four main ways in which a man's honor can be sullied. The first and most obvious way is through one's own dishonorable actions and attitudes. These actions and attitudes may coincide with a moral fault or they may refer to an extra-moral disvalue. In any case, the individual himself is here responsible for the staining of his honor.

The second way is through the dishonorable attitude of another person who is linked to him so intimately that it covers him also with ignominy. A man discovers, for instance, that his father is a thief. He considers himself "dishonored" by this fact.[5] But, patently, the nature of the stain on his honor in this case differs from that of the stain in the former one. In the former case, it is a stain on the "inside" of his honor, i.e., a stain from within. In the latter case, it is a stain on the "outside" of his honor, i.e., a blemish from without. In the first case he feels he is dishonorable; in the second case he only feels dishonored.[6] He considers his social image

[5] Clemens Brentano gives a typical example of such an experience of being dishonored in his novel, *Der brave Kaspar und das schoene Annerl.*
[6] Needless to say, the adequate response to such a tragic fact is deep sorrow over the sin of the father, a concern for his soul, a desire to reform

stained; he realizes that the members of the society in which he lives will rightly despise his father and that this deserved contempt of his father will extend to him.

In order to understand the specific nature of this kind of stain on one's honor it is necessary to keep in mind two features. First, the individual himself is not responsible; the loss of this objective good for him comes as a blow from the outside, as misfortune and not as guilt. The blemish upon the outside of his honor contrasts with the brightness of the inside of his honor. Secondly, he feels he deserves the loss of the esteem of others. The fact that his father is a rascal or a scamp entitles other persons to look down on him. This fact alone suffices to soil his honor, even if no one else ever knew it. The dishonorable action of his father stains his honor because it deprives him of the right to claim respect from others, and because he himself can no longer consider his father as honorable. The brightness of his honor implies that he himself can respect and esteem his father. His own honor and the honor of the family are deeply interrelated; they even flow into each other. The honor of his father is undermined from within by his father's crime. But this stain on the honor of the father does not undermine the son's honor from within; that is, the inside of this shield is not stained by the father's dishonor. Only the outside of this shield is spotted by his father's dishonor.

This kind of spot on the outside of one's honor has a great affinity with the nature of disgrace and shame. We can better understand the nature of this blow coming from the outside, which nevertheless wounds honor so deeply, if we think of disgrace. Certainly the character of being under a cloud as the

---

him, and not primarily the preoccupation with one's own honor and the blow which this misdeed means to one's honor. We prescind for the moment from the fact that the concern with the aspect of dishonor is inadequate because other aspects are incomparably more important. Our present interest is exclusively directed to the different forms in which honor can be besmirched.

result of another's misdeed differs thoroughly from the character of being under a cloud as the result of one's own misdeed. Although in one case there is moral guilt, and in the other, none (thus the two cases are radically opposed), from the point of view of dishonor as well as that of disgrace, they have much in common.

A third way of being dishonored is found in cases in which a wound is inflicted from the outside on one's honor, not only by the dishonorable deeds of closely related persons, but by a specific ignominy visited on oneself. We are thinking above all of the man whose wife betrays him. The cuckold so often laughed at, so often ridiculed, is typically "dishonored." The inside of his honor is not stained, because he is in no way guilty and thus he is not responsible for this tarnishing of his honor. The stain comes from outside. But this case clearly differs from the one in which he discovers that his father is a thief. It would be an inadequate interpretation if one were to say: The dishonorable deed of the wife plays here the same role as the theft on the part of the father in the former case. Much more is at stake in the present case. We have only to compare this case with one in which one's wife is a thief. In the case of the cuckold, something ignominious is inflicted upon the husband quite personally. He is placed in a miserable, ridiculous situation.[7] The misdeed of his wife does not reflect on him; the ignominious situation in which he is

[7] Again we have to stress that to regard such a misfortune from the point of view of honor, and to suffer above all because of the dishonor, is a completely inadequate attitude. Apart from the immorality of the wife, the real evil is her unfaithfulness toward her husband, the desecration of the sanctuary of their love. This is obviously an evil embodying a great disvalue and the loss of a high objective good for him, a good which surpasses by far the rank of honor. Even the public exposure of this desecration, of this intimate wound in his heart, is incomparably more serious than the man's dishonor and much more a matter for worry. We have to stress time and again the relatively low rank of this objective good for the person (honor), and we shall see later on that it is morally inadequate to emphasize the point of view of honor as soon as higher objective goods are in question.

placed differs completely from the ignominy of his wife. It is not the mere shadow of his wife's dishonorable action which spread its darkness over him. The action of his wife is a specific offense against *his* honor.

The shield of honor is injured by such a trial, even if it remains unknown to others, and manifestly all the more if it becomes public. In any case, the ignominy inflicted on the cuckold is another way of tarnishing honor. It is an ignominious role in which someone is placed without being responsible. It is this role, ridiculous and despicable in the eyes of society, tragic in reality, which stains the outside of his honor.

Finally, honor can be assaulted from without by insults, humiliations, and so on. The way in which honor is attacked here differs radically from the first case, the staining of honor by one's own dishonorable deeds, and also from the two abovementioned cases in which dishonor is inflicted from without.

Here there is no question of feeling oneself dishonorable, or even of really being dishonored. The assault on one's honor is experienced as undeserved; indignation is the response in which the brightness of the inside of the shield of honor is contrasted with the outrageous attitude of others. It is a completely different situation. What is here at stake is an offense against honor.

It is in this latter case that conventional elements play a great role. What is considered an offense against honor greatly varies according to different societies and cultural epochs. But whatever may be the token in which the offense is embodied, it always has to be the expression of disrespect or contempt, in short, of an act on the part of others which is meant to attack and offend a man's honor.

In this context we have often mentioned self-esteem and its role for honor. We must now, however, stress that the notion of self-esteem can have different meanings. There is a self-esteem, or rather a self-contempt, which is motivated by moral faults and orientated toward a moral norm. In this sense a man may say, If ever I should betray my friend, I would despise myself, I could no longer have any self-esteem. This man may not be thinking of his honor. He simply wants to express how much he hates betrayal of a friend, how much he grasps the immorality and intrinsic disvalue of such an attitude, and, thus, how much he would find himself hateful and unworthy if he were to do such a thing. Certainly this self-esteem or self-contempt should be something secondary with respect to the *contrition* which is concerned with the moral evil insofar as it offends God. But, patently, this self-esteem is orientated toward the moral norm; and though elements of a subjective emphasis on certain moral values and disvalues may creep in, it definitely has the character of a moral value response.

Quite different from this self-esteem is that which we find in the person who is concerned with his honor. Here it is no longer the true moral norm, but the norm of a certain objective good for the person, his honor, which determines self-esteem. It is the nature of this good, honor, which forms the self-esteem in question. We cannot reduce honor to the mirror of self-esteem, because the nature of this type of self-esteem presupposes honor as the measure. This self-esteem, in contradistinction to the former, is not a moral value response, for it simply derives from the fact that one is able to walk upright, that one possesses an unstained "blazon" or emblem. Sometimes both types of self-esteem are mixed.

In the case of the cuckold, moral self-esteem is in no way affected. But the self-esteem linked to the unstained "blazon" of honor is definitely affected. The ridiculous and ignominious role which stains the outside of the shield of his honor, which deprives him of a certain respect on the part of others, undermines this type of self-esteem. His self-image, therefore, also suffers from this injury inflicted on him.

He also finds that he deserves to suffer disrespect because

of what has happened to him. He feels that, objectively, he has lost the claim to hold an honorable position in society.

We have distinguished between two types of vulnerability with respect to one's honor: vulnerability from within and vulnerability from without. From these two aspects of honor which we have called the inner and the outer, we must further distinguish the mirror of self-esteem and the mirror of esteem by others. The latter two are much more interrelated. Self-esteem, always in the sense of a correlation to honor, is largely orientated toward a measure which is determined by the tradition of the society in which a man lives. A man will consider his honor stained if he has done something which (if known) would deprive him of the esteem of the members of the society in which he lives. His self-esteem depends thus on the potential esteem of other people, or, as we could say, he measures himself with the rule which his society would apply to him.

We see thus that the norm of self-esteem often derives from the norm of esteem by others. Moreover, when we find a spot on the mirror of self-esteem, we are also convinced that we no longer deserve the esteem of others, and vice versa.

The difference between the inside and the outside of honor refers exclusively, however, to the question whether the staining comes from within, through attitudes for which we are responsible, or whether it comes from outside, through attitudes of other persons.

The spot on one's honor due to a dishonorable attitude of the man himself affects self-esteem as well as the potential esteem on the part of others. The spot on one's honor inflicted from without, as in the case of the dishonorable act of a near relative, or in the case of the cuckold, affects our self-esteem, though in a manner completely different from that in which it is affected when the stain is due to a fault of our own. And in the case of a mere attack from without (for instance, insults), neither one's self-esteem nor esteem by the society in which he lives is necessarily undermined.

We see thus that honor is neither a mere fiction nor a mere feeling, but is truly an objective reality. It is a certain objective good for the person which can be damaged from within or from without.

There exist objectively honorable and dishonorable actions, attitudes, and situations. Only things which are objectively dishonorable affect this shield of honor.[8]

The inside of this shield registers with a spot or stain every attitude of man which is objectively dishonorable. The absence of dishonorable things is mirrored in the brightness, i.e., the spotlessness, of this shield. The brightness of honor does not require attitudes endowed with a specific positive value; it suffices for it that nothing dishonorable is done. In fact, the positive quality of what is honorable is much less outspoken and definite than the negative one; it is doubtful whether attitudes endowed with a positive value are mirrored on this shield. Indeed, it may be that positive honorable deeds do not heighten a man's honor save in a different sense of the term.

This shield whose luster depends on self-esteem and esteem on the part of the society in which one lives is the mirror of conduct from the point of view of a certain objective good for the person. As such, it formally differs from moral integrity which mirrors our moral conduct from the point of view of its objective value or from the point of view of its relation to God. It is, further, a mirror for a quality which clearly differs from moral goodness. "Dishonorable" has a certain connotation proper to morally evil attitudes, but it is proper only to some morally evil attitudes, and thus clearly differs

---

[8] However, this applies only insofar as honor is understood within its true and objective limits, and is not extended either to things which are in reality above honor, such as many moral values, or below honor, such as a merely conventional rule.

from immorality as such. Moreover, it is also proper to attitudes which are not morally evil.

After having elaborated the nature of honor we understand better why this shield is also vulnerable on its outside. It is important to repeat once more that different as the stain of a man's honor may be—whether caused through his own deeds or by dirt thrown on it from outside—the brightness of a man's honor requires that this shield be spotless on the outside as well as on the inside.

We already mentioned that the term honor may have different meanings. In order to focus completely on the "honor" which is here our topic, and which has so often been made a substitute morality, we shall briefly contrast it with quite different notions of honor.

We often speak of honoring another person and mean by that a specific form of value response. The outstanding virtues or deeds of a man call for a specific response in which the admiration he deserves finds its exterior expression. This admiration is a kind of reward for his merits; one decorates him, one makes him a member of an illustrious association, one places him on a "throne" on which he deserves to sit because of his merits. The honors granted to someone, which have, patently, a great affinity with glory, are also something intra-human, that is, social, and not metaphysical. But apart from this similarity with honor in our sense, as the shield and emblem of a person, such honors clearly differ completely from it. They are not only manifestly something other than the inside of this shield, but they also differ completely from the outside. The brightness of this shield does not require that a person be honored in the above-mentioned sense. To deserve a normal esteem which allows one to go "upright" through life does not imply that he be honored by others for special feats or merits. It does not imply any exteriorization of a specific admiration, a specific token of admiration, an outspoken elevation. And on the other hand, one's shield of

156 GRAVEN IMAGES: SUBSTITUTES FOR TRUE MORALITY

honor does not become brighter because one has been honored.

Clearly, then, the kind of respect which the outside of this shield requires on the part of other persons does not imply being honored in these special ways and even differs from it. Moreover, in looking on the shield of honor of another person, we are not concerned with the question of "honoring" him. We are thinking not of a "throne" on which he deserves to be placed because of his merits, but of his shield, whether or not it is spotless.

Sometimes "honor" is used in a still more intimate connection with a specific value response than in the case of "honoring" to which we have just referred. In saying, "All honor to this man," honor is the immediate expression of a specific form of veneration. It is not an action by which we express our appreciation; it is not a token of this veneration; it does not have the character of a kind of reward. It is something much higher, the immediate expression, we could say, the utterance of the inner word, of this veneration. It no longer has the social connotation, it has rather a metaphysical character; it is spoken in *conspectu Dei*. The highest type of this meaning of honor is to be found in the liturgy when the priest speaks on the feast of a saint, "... *festum celebrantes sub honore....*"

In the liturgy we find, however, still another notion of honor, in which honor means something incomparably higher. When we hear the words, *"Gloria et honore coronasti eum,"* honor means the "halo," the place granted by God to the saint, the heavenly splendor in which he has been received, as a divine reward. Honor is here a sublime supernatural value, something separated by a world from the shield of honor.

Finally, we find again a completely new meaning of honor when this term is applied to God Himself, as synonymous with *gloria*. *"Omnia ad majorem Dei gloriam"* or *"Gloria honor sit."*

Here the glory and honor of God are attributes of God,

of His infinite goodness, majesty, sanctity; at the same time, honor and glory are the very expressions of our adoring praise, such as in the *"Gloria Patri."*

After setting aside all the different higher meanings of the term honor, we can easily see why honor in the sense in which we have been using it yields itself in a specific way to becoming a substitute morality. Its intrinsic pretension to be the mirror of our dignity and integrity, the shield reflecting whether we deserve self-esteem and esteem by others, predestines it to become a substitute morality. It suffices to follow this pretension, to believe in it, to take it seriously, to let it unfold itself, in order to become prey to a substitute morality. The confusion of the brightness of this shield with moral integrity is thus easily arrived at. And we can see the compromise which has taken place here, since obviously the "unspottedness" of honor appeals to pride and satisfies it. As for concupiscence, it plays no role in the genesis of this substitute.

Now, the deformation found in this substitute morality varies to a great extent according to the things which are considered to be honorable or dishonorable.

We can distinguish three cases. First, honor functions as substitute morality whereby only things are included which are objectively related to honor. On the one hand, morally evil things which have objectively the connotation of dishonorable are considered as morally relevant and, on the other, all the extra-moral things which have the connotation of dishonorable are also considered to be morally relevant. Morality is thus replaced by the authentic notion of honor, i.e., by what honor is in reality.

Secondly, honor as a substitute morality is extended to many moral things which objectively do not have the specific connotation of honorable and dishonorable. In this case, honor is illegitimately elevated.

Thirdly, honor as a substitute morality is extended to

things which are far below the original and true notion of
honor. Here honor is exteriorized and conventionalized.

In the first case, the notion of morally evil is arbitrarily
reduced to those moral disvalues which have the specific connotation of dishonorable. A great part of the moral sphere—
many moral values and disvalues—is ignored and considered
as morally neutral. On the other hand, many extra-moral
values and disvalues are placed on the same level as honorable
and dishonorable things which are morally relevant. This
illegitimate elevation of extra-moral things, apart from being
a grave deformation in itself, is also the reason why many
immoral attitudes are labeled as morally obligatory. Dueling,
for example, is considered a moral duty and the man who
refuses to accept a duel is considered as craven and worthless.
It is here that we find the source of grave sins committed in
the name of honor, and thus considered as morally obligatory.
A father kills his seduced daughter, thereby fulfilling what
he regards as a command of honor, a command which he
considers obligatory, dictated by the norm which has become
a substitute morality.

The deformation found here is both a material and a
formal one. The material deformation goes in the above-
mentioned three directions: first, reducing the moral sphere
to things which have the connotation of honorable or dishonorable; secondly, including in the realm of moral obligation extra-moral and morally indifferent things, because of
their relation to honor; and finally, the grave deformation
which results from considering strictly immoral things as
morally obligatory, because of a true or supposed relation to
honor.

From this material deformation, we must distinguish the
formal one: It consists in the shift from morality with its
intrinsic relation to God and from moral integrity in the light
of God to the shield of integrity as centered in our own self,
that is, to something which is in reality a merely secondary
objective good for the person. It is the disastrous formal per-

version which consists in replacing objective moral goodness, which is pleasing to God, and moral evil, which offends God, with a shield dependent on our self-esteem, and the esteem of the society in which we live.[9] This formal perversion affects inevitably the understanding of every single moral and morally relevant value.

In the case in which honor as a substitute morality is no longer seen in its objective true character (our second case) but is elevated and sublimated—making it coextensive with real moral integrity—the deformation seems much less grave.

True, the material deformation of reducing the moral sphere to the moral values and disvalues which have the objective connotation of honorable and dishonorable is no longer present.[10] Yet if the material deformation is less grave here, the formal deformation is all the graver. Because the more the entire moral sphere is identified with honor and yet not restricted to things which have in fact the connotation of honorable or dishonorable, the more serious is the deformation in approaching the moral sphere under the angle of honor.

The material deformation is patently greatest in the above-mentioned third case of honor as substitute morality, in which the realm of the honorable and dishonorable is widened through a deterioration of the notion of honor rather than through an illegitimate elevation. In this case the realm of honorable covers only a small part of the real moral values, and the extra-moral things which are considered honorable or dishonorable are to a great extent without real relation to the original authentic notion of honor. The entire notion of honor is watered down, superficialized, and conventionalized.

[9] The formal deformation differs, however, from the one we found in tradition as substitute morality. The substitute of honor has always a certain qualitative connotation.

[10] However, he who falls prey to this error will make of honor not a real substitute morality, but an alleged core of morality. He will try to avoid all immoral things, but he will consider the dishonorable as that which must be avoided most of all. Honor will remain the ultimate, privileged norm.

Moreover, many strictly immoral things are regarded as imposed by honor.

Here the formal perversion differs completely from that in the second case. It consists in the fact that a miserable and conventional notion of honor, deprived of its original relative nobility, assumes the role of a substitute morality. Those falling prey to it are conventional, superficial men; and their "honor" is rather ridiculous. They make of this notion which has almost lost all material affinity to moral integrity the norm endowed with some formal features of the moral sphere.

Honor is perhaps the most typical case of substitute morality, not only because it is widespread, but also because the compromise between pride and the value-responding center is especially visible here. Related on the one hand to integrity, with a vague "subcutaneous" relation to the moral sphere, and on the other, predisposed to become a source of satisfaction for pride, it manifestly lends itself in a specific way to the formation of a substitute morality.

We must, however, stress that honor is not only a widespread substitute morality, but very often also an anti-moral idol.

Persons who have a definitely hostile and rebellious attitude toward the moral sphere, and ultimately toward God, may refuse to do things which are against their honor; they are, above all, susceptible to offenses against their honor.

The often quoted "figures" of Don Juan in Mozart's opera, *Don Giovanni,* and Don Rodrigo in Manzoni's novel, *The Betrothed,* are typical examples of this amoral idol of honor. They are always on the *qui vive,* lest anyone attack their "honor." Their every other word is "honor," but they do not admit any moral norm above them; on the contrary, they cynically offend the moral law and show disrespect for all moral values, such as justice, purity, reliability, veracity, not to speak of humility and charity.

For such men honor is completely detached from the above-mentioned immanent vague relation to the moral sphere. It has become the pure exponent of pride. It is a shield whose state indicates whether a man can still be proud of himself, especially with respect to his social image. Honor is reduced to a kind of social standard, the honor of a cavalier as opposed to that of common men. It is completely conventionalized, and is tied in mainly with notions having to do with "good family," a high social class, the possession of wealth.

However, this conventionalized honor still has the character of a shield reflecting some extra-moral values, such as, for instance, courage, audacity, brilliancy.

To lack courage, to yield because of danger, would be experienced as unbearable; it would besmirch the image of himself and make it impossible for one to feel aloof and proud.

Here honor is a shield which reflects not even the self-esteem properly connected with honor, but a kind of esteem which is merely equivalent to a satisfaction of pride, an esteem devoid of all elements belonging to a response to moral values. Also, the self-esteem in question is completely extra-moral and even largely immoral. This is disclosed especially by the fact that immoral elements or moral disvalues, which are recognized as such, are also a source of sustenance for honor. Such people glorify themselves and boast of having seduced a girl, or of having succeeded in deceiving someone, or of having attained their goal regardless of its moral character. They consider it as incompatible with their "honor" to fail in the pursuit of their aims, to yield to anyone else, to accept advice, to submit, to obey, and, above all, to make restitution for some immoral deed, to ask for forgiveness, to have contrition.

It is easy to see that honor here in no way functions as substitute morality; it is clearly opposed to morality even in its most formal features. It never appeals to conscience; it never obliges, morally speaking, but acts exclusively on pride, and influences a man according to the incompatibility of anything with his pride. And pride has already reached in this type such a dominion, in contradistinction to the compromise type, that even extra-moral aspects of moral values no longer attract his pride. Here honor has definitely become an anti-moral idol.

The "honor" of these immoral men is patently a caricature of the original and authentic honor. It is no longer an objective good for the person, but merely something subjectively satisfying, though formally decked out in the robes of an ideal. It possesses this character of an ideal mainly because of the role of the social image. One wants to be respected by others, and inasmuch as these others are not equally immoral, the shadow of an ideal, of something high and praiseworthy, is present. Characteristically enough, those people will consider it as an offense if one charges them with their crimes, though they themselves will glory in them. For the denunciation by others is proffered under a name which reflects disapproval, whereas they themselves call their crime by a glorious name. The moral blame to which as such they are indifferent is, however, an offense to their honor, because it embodies a reason for disrespect on the part of others in their society. Though the content of the blame is of no consequence to them, though it may even be a source of pride, they nevertheless experience blame itself as incompatible with their honor. The fictitious, conventional character of this honor is thus clearly revealed.

We have already mentioned that honor is in fact an objective good for the person, and that in the frame of a merely natural morality it is not only legitimate to appreciate this good, but that it is even an imperfection if one totally disregards it. In order to circumscribe the legitimate role of honor, we want to stress the following facts.

First, no morally evil action or attitude should ever be approached from the point of view of honor. Everything morally evil should be avoided and omitted from the moral point of view, which is intrinsically related to God, and not from the point of view of this objective good for the person. Even if honor does not assume the character of a substitute morality, the very fact that one approaches something morally relevant from the point of view of honor, that is, from its effect on the shield of honor, is already a grave moral deformation. Although certainly the most serious and typical staining of one's honor stems from certain immoral attitudes, it is completely inadequate, to say the least, to approach them under this point of view.[11]

Secondly, with respect to morally irrelevant goods the point of view of honor may be legitimate. It is legitimate to avoid certain actions which, though not morally evil, are incompatible with honor, because of this incompatibility. Again, it is legitimate to approach an evil from the point of view of honor in cases in which the shield of one's honor is spotted from without. But as soon as the event which affects honor is primarily a much greater evil for the person than the loss of honor, it is again a deformation and a completely inadequate approach to look at it from the point of view of honor. It is surely a sign of egocentrism and conventionality to look at a crime of one's own father from the point of view of a cloud on one's honor instead of deploring both the immoral attitude as an offense against God and the evil which the father inflicts on himself. We saw before that the same applies to the man who has been betrayed by his wife. Much higher-ranking goods for the person are here at stake than his honor. To approach it from this point of view would again be a sign of superficiality and conventionalism. Only insofar as an event is in fact exclusively an evil from the point of view of honor is it adequate to approach it from this point of view.

Thirdly, the interest in honor as an objective good for the person should manifest itself in the fact that one is disposed

[11] Needless to say, it is incomparably better if an immoral action is omitted because of honor than if it is accomplished.

to sacrifice it for a higher objective good, while refraining from doing so for objective goods which rank lower.

It is here that the distinction between a man who is under the level of honor and the one who is above this level must be made. The man who is under this level, the really dishonorable man, has a cynical indifference toward this objective good; he lets himself be treated ignominiously for the sake of some profit, he will accept the most humiliating roles in order to attain a goal which satisfies his concupiscence. He will be ready to act as buffoon and may even enjoy letting himself go in this way, and thus giving up a certain dignity. The man who is above the level of honor, on the contrary, will have the freedom of spirit to accept such a humiliating role for the sake of higher goods. He will feel it as a sacrifice, he will suffer in accepting such a role, but he will never be a slave to his "honor" and refuse to accept these offenses against his honor for the sake of a higher good. And the surprising result is that instead of becoming dishonorable, he will become honorable *per eminentiam*. His shield of honor will, objectively, shine in full brightness; or rather, the integrity of his person will be such that to view it under the norm of honor would be nonsensical. He is above the level of honor; and is thus, qualitatively, still further removed from the one who permits himself to be ignominiously treated for gain than the man who cares too much for his honor.

Yet all that we have just said is applicable only within the frame of natural morality. In the life of the true Christian a radically new situation arises. The follower of Christ knows but one glory and one honor: *"Nos autem opportet gloriari in Cruce Domini nostri."*

Humiliations, offenses, ignominy display a completely different aspect in the light of Christ. Not only is the concern with self which is implied in the notion of honor incompatible with the Christian's theocentric attitude; not only is every interest in self-esteem and esteem by other persons absorbed by the question: Does something correspond to the will of

God; is it pleasing to Him, or does it offend God? not only
is the intrinsic false pretension of honor to be the valid mirror
of integrity a horror for the true Christian—but for him to
endure ignominy, humiliation, insults with patience and even
with joy is part of the imitation of Christ: *"Spernere mun-
dum, spernere sperni."*

Certainly he will never sacrifice this objective good of
honor for mere profit's sake. But he will refuse to do so not
because of the norm of honor, but because he does not consider such an attitude in conformity with the will of God. The
baseness of extra-moral dishonorable conduct is shunned by
the Christian because of its moral connotation, or rather,
because the right response to the hierarchy of objective goods
for the person assumes here a new moral significance with
respect to natural morality.[12] Though honor played a great
role in many Christian societies, as we saw in Chapter III,
partly as a relapse into paganism, partly as a remnant of
paganism, partly in a romantic attempt to baptize honor, for
the true Christian, honor should play no role; and for the
saint, honor is never a concern. The true Christian can
never be dishonorable; he is by his very character of disciple
and follower of Christ above and beyond honor; the more
he suffers ignominy and humiliation, offenses and insults,
the brighter will shine the mirror of his true integrity
and dignity: *"Qui se exaltat humiliabitur; qui se humiliat
exaltabitur."*

And yet we must not forget the positive aspect of honor.
Honor is *the* typical interception of the desire in man to live
up to noble and high things. This trend, destined to find its
natural fulfillment in a life on a high moral level (such as

---

[12] We shall see in the last chapter that in Christian morality all those
things which have no moral character, properly speaking, assume a moral
significance. This explains why, for the true Christian, it is not permitted to
let himself be treated shamefully for the sake of some profit. It is not because
his honor will not permit it, but rather because the baseness involved
assumes here a moral significance.

the life of Socrates) and an incomparably higher fulfillment in the *sursum corda* of the Christian, is "intercepted" by honor when it does not find its true fulfillment. This function, however, reveals two very different aspects of honor: on the one hand, an undoubtedly noble element; and, on the other, an egocentric deformation resulting from the fact that a trend noble in itself does not find its true destination. We are now taking honor in its original and genuine sense, and not in a superficialized notion which is already a perversion in the frame of honor itself. Nor are we thinking of an artificial interpretation of the term honor as being synonymous with moral integrity. When we think of a man of honor in the true and genuine meaning of this term, we cannot dispute him a certain nobility. He at least possesses some moral qualities. He has, in fact, a certain tragic character. We could say that the true man of honor always deserves something better than to be a mere man of honor.

Moreover, the fact that in such a man there is a ground capable of supporting true responsibility, and on which one can rely and count, conveys to him an undeniable dignity; and the seriousness with which he takes himself, a seriousness so easily caricatured in the man of honor, is, as such, also an important basis for true morality. It is true that this element is also deformed in the man of honor. But in comparing him with the cynical scapin, we easily grasp this indispensable basis for true morality, even though it is hidden under the veil of this deformation.

The Christian also takes himself seriously; but he does so because God takes him seriously, because he is aware of his character as an image of God and of his destination to attain the *similitudo Dei.*

CHAPTER X

# DISVALUE AND RELATIVE VALUE
# OF THE SUBSTITUTES

SUBSTITUTE MORALITIES are a grave moral deformation and yet they are a *minus malum* compared with amoral and antimoral idols or with complete indifference.

The disvalue of all substitute moralities has been stressed throughout this book. We have dealt not only with the general nature of substitute morality but also with certain concrete instances. It suffices thus to summarize briefly the negative character of substitute moralities.

Insofar as the material, or as we may call them qualitative, substitutes are concerned, we find the following disvalues or elements of perversion. First, every introduction of a material or qualitative substitute is a perversion and deformation, regardless of the specific nature of the substitute. The moral sphere forbids that any other specific value, moral or extramoral, arrogate to itself the place of the general basic value, the morally good. The notion of "morally good" or "morally evil" is an ultimate which allows no other measure to be placed above it as a means of selecting out a segment of the moral sphere as the only valid one. The natural moral sphere reflects God in such a way that it admits only supernatural morality above itself. But as soon as any other point of view, any other norm, arrogates to itself a superiority over the general true denominator of good, a deformation takes place. Even a selection of some moral values as the only valid ones is necessarily a deformation of the moral sphere.

The deformation resulting from any material substitute, whether its content be faithfulness, honor, humaneness and warmth of heart, or self-control, is even more serious and disastrous than a partial moral blindness in a man who is, more or less, morally unconscious. The restriction of morally relevant things and the exclusion of certain moral values due to a substitute imply a deeper deformation than does the incompleteness of the perception of morally relevant and moral values.

We saw before that a material substitute includes in many cases the introduction of an extra-moral value as a moral one, or of an extra-moral aspect of a moral value, and even an identification of this extra-moral value or aspect with moral goodness as such.

It is thus an intrusion of an extra-moral element arrogating to itself the place of moral goodness. An extra-moral element is placed on the throne of morality and invested with the scepter of the moral law. This substitute morality is a mixture of an extra-moral element with the most formal *eidos* of the moral sphere, to wit, its oughtness, its ultimate central position, its relation to our conscience, to responsibility, to guilt and merit. This mixture inevitably implies a general deformation of the moral sphere. This applies both to the case in which an extra-moral value assumes the character of a substitute morality and to the case in which moral goodness is identified with a specific moral value (such as warmth of heart or faithfulness) because of an extra-moral aspect. By the very fact of transposing this moral value from its true position, i.e., as one moral value among many others, to the position of moral goodness as such, i.e., the all-embracing denominator of the moral sphere, a reversal of the true order takes place, resulting in an arbitrary restriction of the moral sphere and an intrinsic falseness which also corrodes the formal character of this morality. Moreover, here too this arbitrary transposition from a specific value to the role of the general denominator is necessarily based on a partial misinterpretation of this value: it is seen in the light of its extra-moral aspects. And this again is rooted in the appeal of this extra-moral aspect to pride or concupiscence. The substitute is a moral evil because it is the result of a compromise between the moral attitude and pride and concupiscence, a compromise which already betrays the pollution of the moral sphere.

Secondly, the substitute always entails a falsification of the entire moral ethos. The degree of this qualitative deformation of the ethos depends upon the specific nature of the substitute. It is not difficult to see that every moral value which a man respects because he believes that his honor imposes him to do so (for instance, faithfulness to his friends, reliability, veracity) is in some way misinterpreted in its quality. The ethos of honor affects every moral value which is respected. The same applies to all material substitutes, such as "warmth of heart," altruism, and others.

This general deformation extends to the perception of every single morally relevant and moral value. But the degree of turbidity of the value perception hinges on the nature of the substitute; and there is a broad scale of opaqueness of the morally relevant and moral values, depending on the nature of each of the various substitutes.

Thirdly, the moral sphere is restricted. Many morally relevant and moral values are not at all grasped, because they are not covered by the substitute in question, that is, they either have no relation to the extra-moral value which is at the basis of the substitute or they do not have its extra-moral aspects. For instance, the adherent of duty, in the above-mentioned sense of a legalistic morality, will not care about compassion, generosity, charity, or purity. Thus the adherent of a substitute is in constant danger of going morally astray, as soon as those morally relevant goods are in question which have no place in the frame of the substitute. For he is necessarily deprived of those virtues which essentially presuppose the grasping of those morally relevant values which are left out here.

Fourthly, in the case of some substitutes, many morally insignificant and neutral things, things that are irrelevant and morally indifferent, are treated as morally relevant.

Fifthly, there exist substitutes in the light of which even many immoral things are presented as morally good, for instance, in the case of honor, dueling, or in primitive tribes, blood revenge.

Let us now turn to the formal substitutes of morality.[1] Here it is the form of the moral authority which is perverted. The formal *eidos* of the moral sphere is deprived of its real absoluteness; it is in some way conventionalized. Even if a tradition, in its content, coincides with the true moral law, the transposition of its intrinsic obligation, its categorical oughtness, into tradition—making of tradition the source of its obligation—is patently equivalent to emasculating the moral norm. Thus in the formal substitute the ethos is infected, not by the quality of an extra-moral value or an extra-moral aspect, but by the formal deformation which replaces respect for the moral law and the response to moral values by mere faithfulness to tradition.

If we prescind from this formal deformation of the ethos, everything depends here upon the content of the tradition. What we have, therefore, is a scale ranging from a materially immoral tradition to a complete coincidence with the true natural law, and even with Christian morality. Thus the qualitative deformation can be immense or it may be completely absent.

Yet one's perception of moral values and one's response to them are in any case deformed and corroded if the norm under which they are approached is tradition. The formal character of every individual concrete value is falsified, its

---

[1] We saw before that in the cases in which the moral law is identified with tradition and morality with faithfulness to tradition, we are confronted with a type of deformation different from that found in the above-mentioned qualitative material substitute.

intrinsic goodness and its obligatory character are more or less overlooked, if one happens to conform to it because it is part of a tradition. The form of every value, its importance-in-itself, is deformed even though the concrete value is affirmed and respected.

Manifestly, one main evil of this substitute is that its completely formal character gives no guarantee whatsoever for the content, the way the qualitative substitute does in both a positive and negative direction. As we have seen, the qualitative substitutes leave out certain moral and morally relevant values, but they also include necessarily other moral and morally relevant values. But in the substitute of tradition the door is open for the intrusion of any possible moral disvalue. Something analogous is found in the formal substitute of "legalism." The man who identifies morality with loyalty to the laws of the state, for whom the moral law is equivalent to state law, also deforms the formal character of morality. But there is still a significant difference, because the formal substitute of "legalism" is not entirely lacking in inner links to the moral sphere. The character of true authority proper to the state, as well as the moral relevance of the sphere of rights, gives to state law a certain relation to the moral sphere which surpasses the one present in the virtue of *Pietät* which the respect for tradition carries forth.[2] Inadequate and false as this formal norm is, it is still not so alien to the moral sphere,

---

[2] There are, however, totalitarian states which are based on a definite anti-moral evil idol, for instance, Soviet Russia and the Germany of the Nazis. In such states, true authority is no longer found, nor is the protection of rights. Yet there exists a subaltern loyalty to the state which survives even when the state has deteriorated to a *latrocinium magnum*. The citizens still adhering to this loyalty are unable to realize that a state could ever be essentially immoral, that it could in reality have deprived itself of all genuine authority. In their subaltern loyalty, they will close their eyes and continue to look at state law as a substitute morality, though it has in reality the character of an anti-moral idol. This was the case with many citizens who were no real Nazis, in Nazi Germany; and is the case with many citizens in Soviet Russia, who are no real communists, i.e., adherents of the anti-moral idol.

especially when it refers more particularly to the penal law in which a moral element is indissolubly contained.

But here also the perception and understanding of morally relevant values are in every single case distorted, even when the state law coincides with the moral law and certain things are stigmatized as evil which are indeed morally relevant disvalues. The identification of the moral norm with state law affects the understanding of every true value, it deprives it of its metaphysical depth, its importance-in-itself. A double reduction is here to be found: First, the equation of moral commandment with a positive commandment, i.e., the reduction of moral values to the type of "superimposed importance" which a positive commandment conveys to something in itself neutral; secondly, the reduction of every valid, positive commandment to state laws. This twofold deformation desubstantializes the understanding of any morally relevant and moral value whatsoever.

Furthermore, the totality of morally relevant values will never be covered; and in addition, morally irrelevant things will be placed on the same level with morally relevant values once they are prescribed by state laws. Again, even immoral things may be presented as "moral" because of the laws of the state. Thus an arbitrary cut-through of the moral sphere takes place, and the "legalist," like the traditionalist, will most likely contradict the moral law in many spheres.

The same applies *a fortiori* to other formal moral substitutes, such as progressiveness or liberalism in which the objective link to the moral sphere is again completely absent.

Apart from these moral evils which are a consequence of the substitute, let us again emphasize that the substitute itself is a general perversion of the moral sphere.

It is not only a screen separating its adherent from true morality, but it permits an extra-moral atmosphere and ethos to creep in. The splendor of the true natural moral values and natural moral law, their noble beauty and grand depth, fades away with the substitute; the breath of eternity, which

Kierkegaard speaks of as the mark of true morality, is replaced by a mere intrahuman atmosphere.

How many people have been led into opposition toward morality by these perversions of morality! How many noble souls have revolted against morality because it was presented to them in the deformation of a substitute! And was it not the noble mission of great moral personalities, such as Socrates, to fight against these substitutes by piercing through to true natural morality?

There can be no doubt that true morality imperatively calls for a cleansing from the perversions resulting from any substitute, and the more so as the substitute recedes qualitatively from true moral goodness. But the abolition of the substitute is desirable only if the substitute is replaced by true morality. If, on the contrary, it is replaced by an anti-moral idol or by a complete vacuum, the last things will be worse than the first.

As mentioned before, the negative character of substitute moralities need only be summarized here. Their relative value, on the contrary, has been less stressed throughout the book. And yet it would be a great and disastrous omission not to emphasize that compared with the various amoral or anti-moral idols or with complete indifference to morality, substitutes still have a positive function, which makes them at least a *minus malum*.

There is no doubt that in comparing from a moral point of view a gangster with a man for whom the notion of honor has become the substitute for morality, and whose desire to remain honorable causes him to abstain from many morally evil things and to respect many morally relevant goods, we prefer that the latter still adhere to a substitute for morality instead of being, like the former, completely indifferent to the moral sphere. Again, in thinking of the bourgeois who identifies the laws of the state with the moral law, we cannot but see that this substitute for morality has at least the function of serving as a protection against many morally bad actions. We could hardly wish that he turn away from this substitute, unless he do so in order to find his way to true morality. As long as he does not find the way to Christ or at least to the true natural moral law, it would in no way be desirable that this substitute be dethroned. Imperfect as it is, wrong and perverted as it is, it still has a positive function, and must be considered at least as a *minus malum*.

The same applies if we compare the adherent of a substitute with the adherent of an amoral idol, for instance, the aesthete. The aesthete may be more attractive in many respects than the bourgeois, the *bien pensant,* or the man who equates moral goodness with loyalty to state laws. He may be more refined, more cultivated, more distinguished. But from the moral point of view, the worshiper of loyalty is definitely preferable. Whereas for the radical aesthete the notion of morally good and evil is void of all meaning and plays no role whatsoever in his life, whereas his conscience is silent and every submission to a norm above himself is alien to him, for the adherent of a substitute morality the notion of morally good and evil still has a meaning in his life, notwithstanding the fact that it is deformed and distorted by a substitute morality.

Different advantages included in the presence of a substitute morality must be distinguished. First, it is always preferable that an immoral action be omitted rather than committed, even if we prescind from the question of motives. It is certainly better that a murder does not take place than that it takes place, not only because the life of a person is spared, but also from the moral point of view. If a man abstains from murdering someone merely because he fears the electric chair, morally insignificant as the motive is and immoral as his attitude may be, it remains true that the grave moral evil of the murder does not come into existence. We can therefore list the mere absence of morally evil actions as the first advantage implied in substitute moralities.

Secondly, in the case in which an evil action is omitted because a substitute forbids it, there is always more than the advantage of the absence of a fully realized morally evil action. The fact that the substitute still includes a link to the moral sphere, that the immoral action omitted is labeled as dishonorable or as disloyalty to the state or as unfaithfulness to tradition, implies a refusal of the immoral action which is not merely accidental. The evil action is omitted because of a value response, an impure one certainly, but still for the reason that one considers it illegitimate, as possessing a disvalue and even a disvalue which has formal moral connotations.

A third advantage which the substitute morality implies, as compared with amoral or anti-moral idols or an absence of any norm, is the eminent function which it performs for the existence and welfare of communities. This is, patently, no longer a moral point of view, but it indicates certainly that from the point of view of goods endowed with a high value, the substitute morality is definitely a *minus malum* or a relative good. Honor, tradition, respect for the laws of the state, the substitute of the *bien pensant* serve as a protection against anarchy, a chaotic disruption or a moral deformation of the family, the state, the nation, and all forms of association.

By that we do not mean that it would not be better for all these communities if, instead of substitutes, the true natural law would rule in them and if, above all, everything would be established in Christ. But it is better for the life and welfare of these communities if at least a substitute for true morality is present than if they were based on anti-moral idols, such as was the case in the Germany of the Nazis, or today in Soviet Russia.

But we need not limit ourselves to a consideration of the omission of evil actions in order to prove that substitute moralities have a relative value or that they are a *minus malum*. For many objectively good actions come out of the adherence to substitute moralities. Certainly it is morally un-satisfactory that a man should be faithful to a friend or keep his promise merely because his honor requires him to do so. But if we compare his attitude to that of the one who does not keep his promise or is unfaithful to his friend, we cannot but admit that even faithfulness for reasons of honor is still an advantage from the moral point of view.

We must realize that, in the case of the substitutes, the coincidence of something praiseworthy from the point of view of the substitute and its morally relevant value is not a com-pletely accidental one, or, as we should express it, it is not a pure coincidence. Some awareness of the morally relevant value or disvalue of the good is still present when it is in-cluded in the commandments imposed by the substitute, some respect for the morally relevant value, some indirect contact.

It is important to stress the positive function which the substitutes perform even though they are deformations and perversions of morality, and despite the fact that they should be abolished in order to give place to true morality. They are an evil without a doubt, but a *minus malum* compared with a moral and anti-moral man. If we consider it important to stress their positive function, it is because many people, in their zeal for true morality, go so far as to regard them as a greater evil than an open rebellion against morality. Espe-cially when confronted with adherents of substitutes which have a bourgeois taint (the substitute of the *bien pensant* or of the "decent" man or of the "loyal" man, loyal in the sense of loyalty toward state laws), the temptation to prefer the "sincere" sinner to them is great. One contrasts the more sincere immoral man with the adherent of a conventional moral norm. One contrasts the "publican" immoral man with the "pharisee" bourgeois, while trying to apply to them our Lord's judgments in the Gospel.

Yet Don Juan is no publican and the adherent to a bour-geois substitute is not necessarily a pharisee. The amoral or anti-moral man in no way feels himself to be a sinner; he therefore stands in radical contrast to the publican in our Lord's parable.

Again we say: The substitutes should disappear, but only in order to give place to the true morality and ultimately to Christ.

## CHAPTER XI

# CHRISTIAN MORALITY

THE ELABORATION of the nature of substitute morality in general and of several concrete substitutes has helped us lay bare the radical difference between moral and extra-moral values. It has led us time and again to focus on the specific nature of morality. On the one hand, the analysis of the substitutes disclosed to us the fundamental qualitative difference between moral and extra-moral values; on the other, this analysis has helped us throw into relief the formal *eidos* of the moral sphere, which is still in some way present in these substitute moralities, in contradistinction to amoral or anti-moral idols.

We mentioned before that the clear distinction of the moral sphere from all other spheres of values, as well as the clear distinction of moral values from all extra-moral values, is one of the most essential tasks of ethics. The elaboration of the specific character of moral values, the throwing into relief of their unique quality, also lays bare, in a specific way, the difference between the morally unobjectionable and the morally good in the sense of a positive moral value.

As long as an ethics is primarily concerned with the morally unobjectionable, instead of centering around the positive moral value, it will never do justice to the very core of morality. And, more especially, it will not be able to do justice to Christian morality; it will not be able to attain the full *prise de conscience* of Christian morality and its difference from merely natural morality. As we have been at pains to show in *Christian Ethics,* our specific aim is precisely this *prise de conscience.* The elaboration of the specific nature of moral values in this volume will serve us anew in throwing some light on several essential features of Christian morality.

The role and character of morality in the various religions cannot be compared with the role and character of morality in the Christian religion. For in the latter, moral goodness and sacredness, that is, the awe-inspiring absoluteness of the divine, are, in a unique way, interwoven in the datum of holiness.

It is not our intention to broach here the vast problem of the role of morality in the different religions.[1] It may suffice to stress that wherever no conception of a personal God is to be found, the notion of an authentic moral obligation, of moral responsibility as well as a call directed to our conscience, seems missing. The formal character of morality is hardly grasped. That does not mean that no concrete moral prescriptions are known. Far from it, for many prescriptions which are, objectively, moral commandments (not to lie or not to kill) are honored, but without a real understanding of their specific moral character. This failure to grasp the specific moral character of these prescriptions betrays itself in three ways. First, these moral prescriptions have often only a hypothetical rather than a categorical character. Instead of the categorical commandment "Thou shalt not kill" of the Old Testament, here the prescription runs as follows: "If thou desirest to ascend in the spiritual order, thou must shun these base things."

Secondly, the notions of good and evil are replaced by the notions of high and low, pure and impure,[2] in which the specific pathos and impact of morality are absent.

[1] This question can be posed in many directions: What is the role played by morality in the immediate approach to life of the adherents of a religion, and how far is morality understood and incorporated in their conscious moral doctrines? We are here primarily concerned with the question how far the datum of moral values is interrelated with the divine and the absolute in the different religious doctrines.

[2] This notion of "pure" is clearly not identical with the moral value of purity. It means rather the spiritual regarded as not contaminated by matter, or by temporal earthly affairs.

Thirdly, these prescriptions which have objectively a moral character are connected to religion in a rather indirect way. They have the role of a "catharsis," which is a mere prerequisite for union with God, with the result that moral life is thereby too easily identified with asceticism and takes on a predominantly negative aspect. Wherever the conception of a personal God is found in some way, positive commandments of a more or less ritualistic sort, imposed by the divinity, may assume the character of moral obligations. But very often, if their fulfillment is looked upon as indispensable, this is because fulfillment is regarded as necessary in order to avoid misfortune or disaster. For failure to obey the commandments may draw down on one's head the wrath of the divinity. The real notion of morality, and therefore of moral guilt and of punishment for moral guilt, is, however, absent. The wrath of the divinity and the misfortunes flowing from it are seen as factual conditions which one cannot afford to ignore.

Certainly moral commandments, that is, obligations resulting from morally relevant goods, are often also included in these religions, but in any case only in function of a prerequisite.

In all religions which stand apart from the revelation of the Old and New Testaments, whether or not they include the notion of a personal divinity and some kind of moral obligation, man's position vis-à-vis morally relevant goods is determined by their role as prerequisite for the religious sphere. The data of "sacredness," of "awe-inspiring," of the supra-rational and mysterious, as properties of the divinity, are not interwoven with real moral values. The link with morality has either the character of merely positive commandments; or, as far as moral commandments are included, moral values do not partake of the datum of "sacredness," but function only as a means, as elements of human conduct, regarded as a presupposition of the religious sphere.

In the Old Testament we are confronted with a completely

new interpenetration of moral goodness and divinity in the conception of God.

Be ye holy, because I the Lord your God am holy....
You shall not steal, you shall not lie nor shall any man deceive his neighbor...Thou shalt not calumniate thy neighbor nor oppress him by violence...I am the Lord.[3]

The same is overwhelmingly revealed in the Decalogue as well as in the teachings of the Prophets.

In the Christian revelation sacredness and moral goodness interpenetrate each other still more intimately in the datum of "holiness." [4] In the Sacred Humanity of Christ this datum of holiness is revealed as something completely new, beyond all possible ideals which a human mind can form. And yet this holiness is simultaneously the fulfillment of all natural morality, its transfiguration.

Holy moral goodness is a very property of God. It is the ineffable goodness of God which is sacred, awe-inspiring, divine. Sacredness is indissolubly linked to moral goodness. Justice, mercy, charity are embodied in the inapproachable majesty of God; and the awe-inspiring glory and majesty, the "sacredness" of God, are essentially and ineffably good. Thus, in the very datum of holiness we find this sacred morality and this moral sacredness.

This interpenetration of morality and the divine entails a completely new thematicity of the former in the life of the

---

[3] Lev. 19:1-21.
[4] We use the term "holiness" for a completely new datum which must be clearly distinguished from the datum of "sacredness." Some notion of sacredness—primitive and distorted as it may be—is even to be found in every primitive natural religion. An enormous scale will be found with respect to sacredness; and, patently, an incomparable datum of sacredness is given in the revealed religion of the Old Testament.

By holiness we mean this unique interpenetration of a completely new moral goodness with this authentic sacredness, found only in the revelation of the Old and New Testaments. We mean by holiness the absolutely new datum of this interpenetration, foreshadowed in the Old Testament, but fully revealed in the Sacred Humanity of Christ.

Christian. Christ and transformation in Christ are the very themes of the Christian's life; and this transformation implies that morality is not a mere presupposition, but an essential element belonging to its very core. Transformation in Christ —the imitation of His Sacred Humanity—is equivalent to the sanctification of which St. Paul says: *"Haec est voluntas Dei: sanctificatio vestra"* (For this is the will of God, your sanctification).[5]

The Christian saint is dominated by one fundamental aim: his love of God. The love of God is the one decisive motive of his life, and this implies two organically united ends. The first is the *similitudo Dei,* the glorification of God through transformation in Christ. The second, the eternal union with God, or the beatific vision.

The fact that Christ and transformation in Him and the eternal union with the Holy Trinity are the primary themes of the Christian's life entails also that morality assume the role of a primary theme.

When Claudel says that no one will ever succeed in making us love morality, but we love Christ, he opposes not only a merely natural morality to Christ, but also a morality which is in some way looked at "from without" and is seen in the light of a code of rigid prohibitions. Misleading as his words are, insofar as they refer to authentic natural morality, he rightly stresses the lovableness of holiness, the intrinsic beauty of the wealth of supernatural virtues in Christ which enchants our heart and which prompts Holy Church to call the Sacred Heart: *"Deliciae sanctorum omnium."*

Yet, granted that the inner aspect of morality is disclosed only in Christ, granted that it is this personal holy Goodness which enchants our hearts, morality itself also becomes lovable in Christ. Granted that it is the absolute Person of the Word which is the theme of the Christian's life, we have to stress that morality has now also become not only a frame of

[5] I Thess. 4:3.

man's life, but its most intimate theme. *Hence the love of Christ implies the love of morality.*

Although it is no longer merely natural morality which is the theme of man's life but rather the holy goodness which is incomparably higher, everything which the natural moral law prescribes and prohibits is also included in holiness. Thus we are entitled to say that because sanctification, that is, transformation in Christ, is the theme of the Christian's life, morality also assumes the character of absolute thematicity.

This incomparable and new thematicity of morality in the Christian's life reveals itself also in this, that the role of morality in all religions which stand apart from the revelation of the Old and New Testaments consists in the fulfillment of certain tangible prescriptions. When certain things are fulfilled, the harmony with the divinity seems assured. In the Old Testament, God says, however: "Be ye holy, because I the Lord your God am holy." And Christ says: "Be ye perfect as your Father in heaven is perfect."

Four marks characterize the completely new situation implied in this commandment. First, we should not only avoid every offense against God by sinning, but strive for the *similitudo Dei*, i.e., the acquisition of a completely positive perfection, holiness. Secondly, this *similitudo Dei* could never be attained by our own forces; it requires grace which we receive as a purely unmerited gift. Thirdly, this *similitudo* implies a continuous co-operation of our free will, i.e., a co-operation which lasts as long as we live. It can never be guaranteed by fulfilling certain prescriptions. Fourthly, the Christian must always feel himself to be an unprofitable servant, even when he has fulfilled all tangible moral prescriptions.

Morality assumes, therefore, not only an absolute thematicity in the Christian's life, but also the character of something which no one, insofar as his own status is concerned, can ever consider himself as having attained. It must confront a man, as long as he breathes, with a task which can never be concluded; and it must lead him on a path on which he must continue to walk, beginning, as it were, every day anew. Thus in the light of what has been said, we can see that the thematicity of morality has three features: First, it is not restricted; secondly, it is always unconcluded; and finally, it is endowed with a fully positive character.

This last-mentioned feature leads us to another mark of Christian morality: With the absolute thematicity is closely connected the predominance of positive commandments at which we hinted in *True Morality and Its Counterfeits*. In natural morality the prohibitions for the commandments to abstain from morally evil actions or attitudes prevail. Even if the formulation is a positive one (for instance, "Respect the property of other persons," "Respect their rights," "Respect above all their life"), the real meaning of these commandments refers to an abstaining from any violation of other persons. The "respect" required would in any case actualize itself in omitting any violation of their rights. The natural moral law imposes, above all, certain limits within which we can move freely. It imposes, above all, the obligation not to show disrespect for any morally relevant good, or to infringe upon it.

Certainly moral obligation is not restricted to mere avoidance of disrespect for morally relevant goods. In many situations, man is called upon to intervene positively. For instance, if another person's life is threatened and if one is able to save him without great risk on one's part, then, clearly, one is obliged to do so.

But the main stress in the natural moral law is nevertheless on abstention from morally evil actions. Even in the Decalogue, prohibition prevails (with respect to the commandments)—only the third and fourth commandment have a positive character, all the others are prohibitive.

We mentioned already in another work [6] that there is an

---

[6] *True Morality and Its Counterfeits.*

objective order, according to which abstaining from moral evil is prior to actions which bring morally relevant goods into existence. The first moral requirement is to abstain from any offense against God. And therefore we must abstain from acting if the realization of a morally relevant good is possible only if we use morally evil means. The unmistakable immorality of the well-known proposition, "the end justifies the means," clearly reveals the primacy of abstaining from moral evil, even when it is hoped that some morally relevant good will result. Yet this primacy does not imply that abstaining from moral evil ranks higher than the realization of morally relevant goods. For this primacy does not have a hierarchical character.[7]

The precedence of abstaining from evil over positive moral actions is not to be found only in the realm of natural morality. The fact that the prohibitions have the character of an

[7] It makes no sense to compare abstention and the accomplishing of morally good actions from a hierarchical point of view. For instance, we cannot pose the question: Does abstaining from murder rank lower or higher than saving another man's life? As long as we do not know why someone abstained from evil, the mere abstention from evil is in itself too indefinite in its positive moral value to be compared with the moral value of a good action.

The primacy in question consists in the fact that the avoidance of morally evil actions is the first thing required; it has rather the character of a minimum. But it is a minimum which can never be compensated for by any other morally good action. Failure to fulfill this minimum in one place cannot be redeemed by doing other good actions.

This minimum has the character of a first irreplaceable requirement. It is better to fulfill this minimum than to do many other good actions while failing to fulfill this minimum. In every case in which something positively good (charitable aid, undoing an injustice) could be accomplished only through an immoral means or through doing simultaneously something morally wrong, we should abstain from any action and not intervene. Man's mission to intervene must not be overestimated. As long as he can realize a morally relevant good only in realizing simultaneously a morally relevant evil, he must abstain from any intervention, granted that both are on the same level. And in the case where the morally relevant evil is such that the action realizing it is a sin and is forbidden by an absolute veto, man must abstain from any intervention, whatever may be the rank of the good in question.

indispensable minimum applies also to Christian morality and is therefore in no way characteristic of natural morality. To abstain from sinning has in Christian morality the same precedence over positive moral good actions as in natural morality. It is equally imperative in Christian morality to abstain from any action when the realization of a morally relevant good could be attained only by a sin.

In Christian morality, abstaining from sin assumes the character of a positive expression of the love of God, and is the very first obligation which we should fulfill. Thus the prohibitions of the Decalogue are not relaxed by the two commandments of Christ, but are rather included in them.

We must distinguish between the following two differences: on the one hand, the difference between abstaining from sin and the realization of morally relevant goods; and on the other, the difference between the mere absence of moral disvalues and the presence of moral values. If either the abstaining from sin or the fulfillment of what a prohibition requires is a merely objective fact involving no obedience to the moral law, it guarantees only the absence of certain moral disvalues. But as soon as this abstaining from sin is the result of obedience to the moral law, it becomes the bearer of a positive moral value along with any action which flows out of it.

We must not identify abstaining with the mere absence of a moral disvalue, and restrict the presence of a moral value to positive actions and positive interventions. The difference between the mere absence of moral disvalues and the presence of moral values finds its expression in terms of what is simply morally unobjectionable and what is positively good morally. But the purposive abstaining from sin is a bearer of a positive moral value and is not a mere matter of avoiding the morally objectionable. The prohibitive moral commandment also appeals, as such, to an act of obedience which is the bearer of a positive moral value.

We stress the prevalence of prohibitive commandments in natural morality in contradistinction to Christian morality for other reasons. It is, first of all, the absolute thematicity of morality in the Christian's life which discloses itself in the prevalence of positive commandments. The morally unobjectionable is absorbed into the morally good: the saint approaches life no longer merely from the point of view of the morally unobjectionable, but from the point of view of the morally good by which God is glorified. Here we need only recall the abyss which separates the *similitudo Dei* from the morally unobjectionable.

Secondly, the emphasis on positive commandments manifests the above-mentioned unlimited scope of morality. The love of God does not aim only at fulfilling the obligatory (which is always linked with avoiding sin) but at imitating Christ and, manifestly, such imitation surpasses the mere fulfillment of obligatory commandments. The Christian remains concerned with the moral sphere in every situation, whatever its specific character may be, because his continuous striving to follow Christ and to accomplish everything in His spirit implies throughout the moral theme.

On this background, we easily understand why in Christian morality the predominance of prohibitions with respect to positive commandments is no longer to be found: The two commandments of Christ which "embrace the whole law and the Prophets" are univocally positive. So also are the Beatitudes.

We come now to a third and new characteristic of Christian morality: the extension of moral relevance or the penetration of the moral theme into all domains of human life.

The basic relation to God, through Christ, with Christ, and in Christ, gives to all domains of life, to all activities, an indirect moral relevance. The basic bond to God, the *religio,* filling the entire life of man with the great preoccupation of fulfilling God's will in everything, bestows on every type of human activity the character of moral responsibility and of a certain moral relevance.

The first general thing which we have to state concerning

the extension of moral relevance is the fact that because man
is not his own master, but only God's steward, moral responsibility is extended to many spheres which are by their
nature extra-moral.[8] If, in the frame of natural morality, a
poet, a scientist, or a philosopher wastes his talents, if instead
of unfolding them and making valuable contributions, he
dedicates most of his time to other activities (for example,
sport, social affairs, and traveling or even such a noble thing as
the enjoyment of beauty in art and nature), we may blame
him and deplore this waste. But we cannot consider him morally guilty. A clear frontier divides the waste of cultural
talents from acts of injustice, cruelty, hardheartedness, or impurity. Whereas the latter implies a grave moral guilt and
moral disvalues, the waste of one's cultural talents remains
merely a matter for pity and shame.

The profound difference between these two domains certainly subsists in Christian morality. Yet the waste of talents
also assumes here a moral relevance. The right use of talents
entrusted to man by God, talents which man possesses not as
an owner, but only as a steward, has become a matter of conscience. He is responsible for them before God. The parable
of the talents in the Gospel refers, it is true, primarily to the
gifts of grace, but it must analogically be extended to all
natural gifts.

Something analogous may be said concerning the attitude
toward one's own health. In the frame of natural morality,
one cannot strictly say that the man who does not take care of

8 The notion of responsibility is sometimes identified with moral responsibility. Yet if it is true that only acts for which we are in some way responsible
may be bearers of moral values or disvalues, not everything for which we
are responsible has a moral connotation in the frame of natural morality.
We may also speak of responsibility in all cases in which something depends
upon our free decision, even if the content of this decision is not morally
relevant. If in a restaurant I choose to eat pork cutlets and not veal cutlets,
I am responsible for this choice in the sense that it was in my free power
to choose. But the object of the choice is such that in itself it has no moral
connotation. Clearly we are here interested only in responsibility in the full
sense, that is, moral responsibility.

his health is stained with moral guilt. But in Christian morality, man is also responsible for disregarding this gift of God. Like everything else he possesses, his body is not his own property, but God's. Here he is also but a steward. True, he may be called by God to sacrifice his health for the realization of high morally relevant goods—for instance, as missionary— or in emergency situations in order to help other persons physically or morally. But he becomes morally guilty if he ruins his health merely out of thoughtlessness and by following his moods. Many things which are left to the free choice of man in natural morality, such as a profession, become subject to a kind of moral responsibility in Christian morality. The Christian should choose the profession which, he believes, is in accord with God's loving plans. Certainly, one's affinity with a profession and his natural propensity for it, one's talent and the delight one finds in it, must be considered as indications of God's will. But the very fact that the decision is taken from the point of view of God's will gives to it a completely new character of moral responsibility. What was merely "left up to the person" to decide, to his own advantage or damage, but without moral responsibility, assumes now a moral connotation by the very fact that one is responsible to God for the right decision.

Whereas this extension of moral responsibility pervades the Christian's entire life, as a general feature, the nature of moral relevance manifests itself in a great variety of ways in the various spheres of activity. This variety is due partly to the nature of the sphere of activity in question, partly to the nature of the act by which we link it with God. It ranges from a moral relevance which is merely indirect to acts which are bearers of a definite moral value.

It is not our intention to consider here all the ways of linking the different realms and actions of man's life to God. We only want to enumerate some main types which may illustrate this extension of moral relevance.

First, there are many occasions in which a positive linking

of an activity to God is not the question, for what concerns us is the attitude of *religio* in which we have to remain during this activity. This is, for instance, the case with respect to many everyday activities such as washing, dressing, driving a car, in short, every situation which may draw us into a peripheral level of our soul or distract us. Here remaining united with God rather runs parallel with the respective activity; the theme of the activity is not linked with God.

Secondly, the true Christian encloses many spheres within a sacred rampart, especially those in which concupiscence can easily intrude. Take eating, for example. In the frame of natural morality, eating may be an occasion for displaying moral disvalues, such as, for instance, gluttony. But eating in a normal, healthy way is not a bearer of positive moral values. Keeping our bodily instincts under control [9] through moderation is certainly praiseworthy first of all because of the absence of moral disvalues resulting from a yielding to concupiscence, and secondly, because of a positive extra-moral value which constitutes a certain "spirituality." However, this moderation is not yet a positive moral value in the strict sense of the word. But in Christian morality, eschewing self-indulgence for the sake of remaining in the frame of *religio* definitely becomes the bearer of moral values.

Not only is the yielding to concupiscence a much greater evil in Christian morality, but the act of the Christian by which he gains a secure footing within this rampart in order to counteract the danger of concupiscence, and to prevent him from slipping out of the sphere of the *religio,* is itself a bearer of positive moral values.

We need only realize that according to Christian doctrine soul and body receive through Baptism the new dignity of being temples of the Holy Ghost in order to understand the duty of erecting a rampart against all concessions to concupis-

[9] Manifestly we are not thinking here of the sexual sphere. The unique character of this sphere which separates it clearly from all other instincts, has been analyzed in our book: *In Defense of Purity*. Sheed and Ward.

cence. Yet it must be emphasized that it is never the act of eating as such which is the bearer of a moral value, but rather the attitude which accompanies it, that is, the erecting of a rampart.

Something analogous is to be found in the rampart which protects us from pride. In order to remain in the frame of the *religio* during all activities, and not to be held by the fetters of pride, we set up a holy rampart with our will. This act is definitely the bearer of positive moral values.

A third extension of moral relevance in Christian morality results from the role of thanksgiving in the Christian's life. Every good which the true Christian receives leads his mind to God and engenders an act of thanksgiving, because he knows that all goods are gifts bestowed on man by God's bounty. Hence, while the holy rampart does nothing more than surround fruitions and activities, the act of gratitude with which everything is accepted (from the food we eat to the beauty of nature and art) pervades the respective fruition with a new ethos.

The thanksgiving which we find in the Liturgy as well as in the lives of saints is a direct value response to God's infinite bounty and is thus a bearer of a specific and genuine high moral value.

Nevertheless, there is clearly a difference between a fruition pervaded by an act of gratitude and an act which on the natural level is already a moral one.

It is neither eating as such nor the delight over the beauty of nature which embodies a positive moral value, but rather the act of gratitude which accompanies it. The act of gratitude which is the bearer of a moral value has here a merely accessory character; it is an accompanying factor, one that is added to the enjoyment of the respective good. If a Christian did not enjoy a good because of some insensitivity, he would not be morally guilty; but if he did enjoy it and were not grateful to God, he would at least be stained by a moral imperfection.

Gratitude toward God for receiving one good or another from His bounty—from the most modest to the highest—apart from being the bearer of a moral value, certainly has also a bearing on the character of the fruition or enjoyment. But this fruition itself never becomes thereby a bearer of moral values. It only acquires an indirect moral connotation.

In his relation to many goods endowed with a high value, such as nature and art or loved ones, the Christian not only links his enjoyment of beauty and his love of persons to God by an act of gratitude, but he loves them in God. This *amare in Deo* implies several elements which vary according to the high good in question, and among them the reverent, grateful attitude is indispensable. As for beauty, the Christian also finds God in it in some way, perceiving it as a message from above. And in the case of loved ones, his approach to them is characterized by the desire to find and meet them in Christ. Later on we shall come back to it more in detail; here it may suffice to stress that this *amare in Deo* possesses a moral significance.

Again, a morally unobjectionable activity assumes moral relevance when it is accomplished *ad majorem Dei gloriam*. This applies to different forms of professional work. Activities which in themselves are not bearers of a positive moral value, such as, for instance, the creation of a work of art or a philosophical or scientific work, will be endowed with moral significance when accomplished with this intention. Analogously, this intention can be applied to every morally unobjectionable work; but, patently, not to every unobjectionable activity. It must be an activity which by its very nature lends itself to such an intention.

The intention of accomplishing an activity *ad majorem Dei gloriam* is an actualization of our love of God. As such, this intention is definitely a bearer of a moral value. But the activity in question assumes only an indirect moral relevance.

A special case in which an extra-moral sphere receives

moral significance through this intention is the endurance of pains or trials. To endure them is, as such, not morally relevant; but it becomes a bearer of moral values if it is offered to God. To endure physical pains courageously, instead of doing so in a wailing manner, is certainly praiseworthy, but it does not yet embody a specifically moral value. To endure courageously all kinds of trials certainly deserves our admiration, but it cannot be considered a bearer of a moral value in the full sense of the word. But as soon as physical suffering or other crosses imposed on us are offered to God, this endurance assumes a high moral value.[10]

However, the fact that every domain of the Christian's life assumes an indirect moral relevance in no way effaces the difference between the sphere which is by its very nature essentially moral and the spheres which are, as such, extramoral. The decisive change taking place in Christian morality does not in the least imply that all different domains of life are leveled from the point of view of moral significance. The primacy of morally relevant goods remains untouched, but a certain indirect moral relevance is extended to all other spheres whose moral relevance remains nonetheless incomparable with the sphere which is by its nature essentially moral. In all these other spheres, moral relevance is indirect and never touches the very core of morality, as we shall see later on.

We are here confronted with a mysterious paradox: on the

---

[10] Certainly, on the level of natural morality, it is also a morally good attitude if someone endures physical pains and mental sufferings with patience and abstains from irritation and unfriendliness toward the persons surrounding him. The fact that the positive responses to other persons remain undisturbed by suffering, that he does not make others suffer, or that he does not importune them, manifests certainly an attitude which is endowed with a moral value. It is not difficult, however, to see that the moral value of enduring pain and suffering—when the endurance is offered to God—has a completely different character. This value is independent of the behavior toward the persons surrounding the one who suffers; it is also present if someone suffers in complete solitude; and it is a value which is much more proper to the enduring as such.

one hand, only in Christian morality is the very core of morality disclosed, and yet, on the other, all extra-moral spheres become morally significant. Thus the distinction between the moral sphere and all the extra-moral spheres is brought to the foreground, and at the same time, the latter are brought into a vital relationship with morality. Let us understand this clearly. We said in *Christian Ethics:*

A third mark of Christian morality is the fact that here this specific goodness of charity is its very core, whereas in natural morality rectitude, uprightness, and justice are its very core. For instance, Socrates' personality emanates a spirit of veracity, sobriety, rectitude, justice. But St. Stephen's prayer for his murderers exhales the superabundant goodness of charity. And in St. Francis of Assisi's embrace of the leper there shines forth the same luminous, irresistible charity. But, above all, this holy goodness of charity is embodied in the words of our Lord: "Love your enemies: do good to them that hate you." [11]

This implies also a univocal distinction between the moral sphere and all extra-moral spheres. The difference between all extra-moral values (such as courage, self-control, efficiency, assiduity, parsimony, and moderation) and moral values (such as justice, purity, generosity, humility, and charity) goes hand in hand with the disclosure of the very core of morality and with the throwing into relief of its very spirit.[12]

The words of Christ, "What doth it profiteth it a man to gain the whole world . . . ," while revealing the incomparable priority of moral values over all other values, and simultaneously the fact that moral perfection is the one absolute good for the person, imply also the decisive difference between moral values and all extra-moral values. The unique qualita-

[11] *Christian Ethics*, pp. 461-462.
[12] Something analogous applies to the difference between all extra-moral goods (such as art and science, or fame, glory, and success) and the goods that are morally relevant (such as, for instance, the life of other persons, their welfare and their rights).

tive character of moral values, the matchless seriousness of morally relevant goods, as against all other values and goods, clearly shines forth in these words of our Lord.

But while the distinction between moral and extra-moral values is here thrown into relief in an incomparable and un-forgettable manner, and the difference between the morally unobjectionable and what is positively good morally is more strongly emphasized than anywhere else, nevertheless all extra-moral spheres assume a moral significance in one way or another.

Insofar as the nature of the goods is concerned, the difference between moral and extra-moral shines forth in an unprecedented clarity; but insofar as everything is seen in the light of God and our *religio,* and insofar too as our whole attitude is pervaded by the love of God, all extra-moral goods assume indirectly a moral significance. This new moral significance of extra-moral spheres has the same root as that new thematicity of morality of which we have already made mention. Both are the consequence of seeing everything in God and in the light of God, and of living within the bounds of *religio.*

At this point we must utter a warning against a dangerous misinterpretation of the linking of all these extra-moral spheres with God. Sometimes the manner of relating everything to God and of permeating every sphere of life with the love of God is falsified, an artificial superimposition takes place which frustrates the natural theme of the various goods and the immanent logic of their use or enjoyment.

If, for instance, someone while about to fall to sleep should direct himself to God in a cramping tension of his will in order to be united with God in the moment of falling asleep, he may frustrate its immanent process. Or, if in hearing beautiful music, instead of yielding to its beauty, one should exhaust all his spiritual energy in a paralyzing tension of linking from without this experience to God, the enjoyment may be frustrated. Whether it is thanksgiving for the enjoyment or the use of any objective good for us, or the accomplishing of our work *ad majorem Dei gloriam,* or whether it is the erecting of a rampart around the field of the agreeable against the intrusion of concupiscence, these acts should always be organically connected with the natural theme of the object and must never assume the character of a cramping intervention of our will which paralyzes and frustrates our natural activity.

Thus the link to God in thanksgiving differs from the link to God that is present when one erects a rampart around the agreeable; both these links differ from that of the *amare in Deo,* just as all these differ from that of the *ad majorem Dei gloriam.*

This danger is especially acute in the case of the *amare in Deo,* that is, the incorporation in Christ of the fruition of a good endowed with a high value. In enjoying the beauty of nature or a work of art, the incorporation of this attitude in Christ does not imply that the beauty is no longer the theme or that, in linking it with God, one interrupts and undermines the immanent logic of "drinking in" this beauty.

The transfiguration which should take place here and which is the soul of this new moral significance is, on the contrary, based on a new vision of all the extra-moral goods and man's entire life. Thus the link with God is not the result of an artificial superimposition by our will, for high extra-moral goods disclose in the *lumen Christi* the message from above which is intrinsically included in their own specific value.

Beauty in nature and art, beauty of visible and audible things, is grasped by St. Francis as a message from God, as a mirroring of God's and Christ's infinite Holiness, and thus is seen in its congeniality and affinity with the world of moral values. This vision, manifestly, does not efface visible and audible beauty, it does not deprive it of its very theme. On the contrary, this vision in which the *implicit* qualitative message, already present in the merely natural approach, becomes an *explicit* one gives to beauty its highest fulfillment.

The same applies to loved ones. In seeing them in their character of images of God and destined to attain the *similitudo Dei,* the charm and beauty of their personalities, instead of fading away or of being clouded over, are disclosed in a specific way and assume a new and greater splendor. In seeing them as beloved by Christ and redeemed by Him, our love for them, far from becoming less personal, is directed to those very personalities in an incomparably deeper way.[13]

We are here confronted with the mystery which finds its most typical expression in man himself. The more a man can say, "And I live, now not I, but Christ liveth in me," the more lovable will he become in himself, and the less apt to be regarded as a mere transition point, that is, a mere means of loving God. Thus we confront anew the truth that God is closer to us than we are to ourselves.

Analogically, every high natural value, far from becoming a starting point for meditating about God, is resplendent with a new and incomparably higher preciousness when seen in the *lumen Christi.*

On the basis of the transfiguration which has taken place on the object side, we can more readily understand how the relation to God in our attitude differs from any superimposed direction of the good to God. This will become clearer after having contemplated some features of the *amare in Deo.* The incorporation into our religious life of the fruition or enjoyment of loving and being loved, or the fruition or enjoyment of beauty in nature and art, implies a kind of sanctioning of our "being affected" and of our value response. Certainly, it is not the strict kind of sanctioning which is possible only with respect to morally relevant goods.[14] Still, it is in no way a mere *nihil obstat* given by our free spiritual center. In

---

13 We prescind here from charity or the love of neighbor, because this kind of love *a fortiori* presupposes the love of Christ. Our topic here is the change which parental or filial love, friendship or conjugal love, undergoes when the person is loved in Christ.

14 Cf. *Christian Ethics,* Chapter 25.

*Christian Ethics,* we distinguished moral sanctioning from a mere *nihil obstat:*

We distinguished the sanction from any mere "let it be," which endorses something in giving free rein to its development, analogously to the "let it be" granted to the satisfaction of bodily instincts or urges. But such an endorsement of joy at winning a game of chess, or a tennis match, is in no way a solemn identification of our free spiritual center with this joy. It is in no way a forming of this joy from "within," which grants to it a new significance.[15]

The sanctioning proper to the *amare in Deo* has this in common with moral sanctioning, that it is a "solemn" yes, entailing a specific full participation of our person in the value response or fruition in question. It is also like the moral sanction in that the free spiritual center does not remain "outside," merely allowing, as it were, something to take place, but it enters into the very marrow of the value response or fruition; the free spiritual center forms it from within. As for the difference between this sanction and the moral sanction, it is to be found in the fact that the "yes" of the free spiritual center does not have the character of a co-operation with the oughtness proper to the moral sphere. In the case of the sanctioning of a response which is morally called for, or of the disavowal of a morally evil response such as envy or malicious joy, the "yes" or "no" is a strict counterpart of the moral oughtness embedded in the morally relevant value.[16] Thus moral sanctioning has, in relation to the oughtness, a complementary character which is not present in the sanctioning of extra-moral value responses nor in the fruition of high extra-moral goods.

The nature of this extra-moral sanctioning clearly reveals

---

15 *Christian Ethics,* p. 330.

16 This oughtness is, however, not restricted to the case of obligation; it is to be found also when an invitation referring to something morally good is at stake. All morally good acts have the character of this unique oughtness. They should come into existence as something morally good.

the difference between true *amare in Deo* and artificial super-imposition. Let us take the case of conjugal love. The *amare in Deo*, the sanctioning of this love for a creature in *conspectu Dei*, the transformation of this love by incorporating it in the love of Christ, in no way deprives this love of its spontaneous rhythm, its enchantment, its ardor and immanent logic. On the contrary, far from depriving this love of all these features, it increases and enhances them by elevating this love to a higher level, and by giving to it an unsuspected depth.

What matters in our context is to understand that the sanctioning of such extra-moral value responses and fruitions does not have the character of something artificially superimposed by our will.

But the artificial superimposition of our will is not the only possible misinterpretation of the sanctioning of the fruition of high goods or the sanctioning of extra-moral value responses. Sometimes one falls prey to another grave misinterpretation, even while anxious to ward off the danger of frustrating the fruition or the immanent logic of these experiences by an artificial superimposition of the will. One believes that the integrity of the immanent logic and the specific natural theme can be preserved only by restricting oneself to a mere *placet* (let it be) from without, thereby allowing the respective experience to develop itself in its immanent logic.[17] It is thought that as soon as something is seen to be morally unobjectionable and even according to God's will, one should let it unfold exclusively in its immanent logic. One argues: Nature is created by God, and we must allow it its rights; we remain therefore in union with God by the very fact that we accept this, our earthly condition, as something God-given. Hence, it is concluded, one does not need to erect a rampart and still less does one need to form the respective activity through a specific act directed to God. Wrong as this conclu-

[17] Artificial superimposition was primarily the danger since Jansenism, whereas today we often encounter the latter error.

sion is, in general, it becomes absolutely disastrous when applied to the *amare in Deo.*

In the case of activities like games or sports, a mere *placet* is insufficient from the point of view of remaining in the bounds of *religio,* and sometimes also from the point of view of an immunization of these activities by means of the rampart. But in the case of high goods which call for an *amare in Deo,* a mere *placet* would be radically inadequate from the point of view of the value and meaning of these experiences. Here a sanctioning is called for which elevates and transfigures the natural experience. As we saw before, the incorporation of parental, filial, conjugal love for friendship into Christ, far from consisting in a mere *placet,* changes them from within—not by lessening their ardor, not by frustrating their immanent logic, but by transfiguring and elevating them. The higher the natural value of an experience is, the more it lends itself to a transfiguration in Christ. To believe that the higher the value of a creature ranks, the more it should be left to his immanent logic, is wrong. The higher its value ranks, the more our relation to it (in the present existential order, and after the transfiguration of the world by Christ) calls for an elevation by Christ and in Christ.

Thus the apparent respect for the natural value which interprets the sanctioning as a mere *placet* is in reality a refusal to grant these high goods the privilege of being transfigured through access to the world of Christ. As we can see, this attitude is not the real antithesis to the artificial superimposition which denies to the natural sphere any right in Christian life. The artificial superimposition replaces the natural theme by something else; it frustrates and even ostracizes it, as it were. On the other hand, to recommend a mere *placet* with respect to these high goods, though granting them a full place and right in man's life, is to do so at the cost of the dignity and rank of their role. One affirms them, and yet, in a deeper sense, one does not, inasmuch as they are regarded as not worthy of being transfigured and incorporated in the supernatural life.

Summarizing, we may say: The extension of moral relevance and significance in Christian morality, which never effaces the difference between morally relevant and morally irrelevant goods, manifests itself in the following ways.

First, the Christian's position with respect to extra-moral goods is submitted to a moral responsibility through his relation to God. Since, at all times, he is but a steward and never the absolute owner of God's gifts, he is responsible for his attitude to all goods, even if they are morally irrelevant. To fail as steward in the use of morally irrelevant goods is certainly radically different from any failure with respect to morally relevant goods and always remains so. However, through the general responsibility toward God, the Lord and Donor of all goods, extra-moral spheres assume a moral relevance, but a moral relevance which is indirect rather than direct.

Secondly, extra-moral spheres become the seat of acts which are bearers of moral values. This fact is linked to the above-mentioned absolute thematicity of morality in the Christian's life. The superactual [18] *religio* and the superactual love of God actualize themselves in situations which are, as such, extra-moral; and it is obvious that every act which is an actualization of man's reverent obedience, his bond of *religio,* and especially his love of God, is an eminent bearer of a moral value. Thus the erection of a rampart against the intrusion of concupiscence, still more, every act of gratitude to God, and finally the offering of any work or of one's physical pains to God are bearers of moral values. They have not only an indirect moral relevance but they are endowed with a definite moral value. But even here the situation remains a very different one from that in which goods are in question which are by their very nature morally relevant. The fruition or enjoy-

[18] Cf. *Christian Ethics,* Chapter 17, p. 241 ff.

ment of an objective good for the person, for instance, a beautiful journey or a restored health, is itself not something morally relevant. It is not this enjoyment which is a bearer of moral values, but rather the act of gratitude; this act of gratitude elevates this enjoyment, enlightening it, as it were, ennobling it, thereby giving it a certain indirect moral significance.

It must, however, be stressed that this indirect relevance has a completely different character from that which any object may acquire by being used as a means of bringing a morally relevant good into existence.[19] Nor is it the indirect relevance due to circumstances which is here in question.[20]

Again, this indirect relevance is not the moral relevance which something assumes because of a specific motive. If someone destroys a growing thing (a plant or a flower) in order to satisfy an evil desire for destruction, this action would be morally evil, though destruction of a plant is not, as such, a morally relevant action. Here something in itself morally irrelevant becomes morally relevant because the attitude which motivates this action is morally evil.

In the cases of indirect moral relevance which we find in Christian morality, the morally good act is not the motive of our activity. Clearly, the erection of a rampart does not have the character of a motive, nor has gratitude, nor the act through which the love and fruition of natural goods endowed with a high value is transformed into an *amare in Deo*.

It must further be stressed that the indirect moral relevance in Christian morality implies not only a moral connotation, but a connotation of supernatural morality. The extension of moral relevance implies the relation to this completely new, transfigured morality with all its incomparable sublimity.

---

[19] Quinine is, as such, a morally irrelevant good; but because of its function as a means of fighting malaria, it acquires an indirect moral relevance.

[20] To waste water is morally irrelevant, but during a period of water shortage, it acquires a moral relevance.

We now can clearly see why the extension of moral relevance in no way effaces the difference between extra-moral goods and morally relevant goods. It not only presupposes this clear-cut difference, but in giving to extra-moral goods an indirect moral relevance, it in no way makes less visible the difference between morally relevant and morally irrelevant goods.

The difference between moral and extra-moral values remains fully present to the Christian conscience, and far from being diminished, shines forth in absolute clarity. The extension of moral relevance in no way brings extra-moral courage closer to justice or purity. On the contrary, in the light of Christian morality, the distance between extra-moral courage and any moral virtue (such as justice, purity, or generosity) is thrown into relief in a most outspoken way, as we have stressed above.

The fact that only in Christ does the difference between moral and extra-moral values shine forth in full clarity discloses that even natural morality is fully laid bare only in Christ. The very core of morality is revealed and sharply thrown into relief against all extra-moral values. And thus, only in Christ, can all substitutes be unmasked.

Certainly, more important still is the revelation of the completely new holy morality in the Sacred Humanity of Christ. But it must also be emphasized that in Him all distortions of natural moral values are unveiled, for Christ has also cured and restored man's perverted nature. Here, we can aptly apply the words, "Seek ye first the kingdom of God and His justice, and the rest will be added unto you." With the incomparably higher gift of supra-natural morality a pure view of natural morality is restored; and in the light of Christian morality, centered around holiness, the devil's hand in all substitutes is unmasked.

As a general principle, it must be said that the lower being, which is in a specific way related to a higher one, also becomes more intelligible in the light of this higher being. This principle finds its highest fulfillment in the fact that the created world discloses its real depth and meaning only in the light of God. This applies again in a new way to the relation between revealed truth and the knowledge accessible to our reason. Creation, the world, man, life, the sphere of values, all become more intelligible, disclose their ultimate nature and meaning in the light of Christ: *"In lumine tuo videbimus lumen."*

Thus, once Christian morality and the absolutely new splendor of holiness have been revealed to us, once from "His Brightness, a new light hath risen on the eyes of our souls," we also recognize in true natural morality "The Voice of the Beloved."